CHARLOTTESVILLE

COMMONS

2013

PHOTOGRAPHERS

Andrea Hubbell + Sarah Cramer Shields

EDITOR

Jenny Paurys

WELCOME TO THE INAUGURAL EDITION OF *COMMONS*, A COLLECTION
OF PHOTOGRAPHS, STORIES, ESSAYS, AND RECIPES FROM THE FOOD
COMMUNITY SURROUNDING CHARLOTTESVILLE, VIRGINIA.

While this publication found its way into the hands and homes of our friends and neighbors in fall 2013, it found its genesis during a trip we took in early 2012 to New Orleans, a city known for its iconic culture and food. As professional photographers with a genuine love of food, we were enthralled with the rich sense of place we found in every dish we ate there. We knew our own city, Charlottesville, had its own food stories and culture to share, and when we returned home, we set about documenting those stories in a web-based passion project dubbed Beyond the Flavor.

The more people we met and the more stories we told, the more we understood the collaborative nature of our local food community, built through the talents and toil of farmers, chefs, artisans, food enthusiasts, growers, bakers, and regular folks, all striving toward a goal of feeding their neighbors and themselves with fresh, high-quality food grown, raised, and crafted right here amid the rolling hills and red soil of Central Virginia.

From the moment we conceived of this project, we envisioned not only a website, but a publication, something tangible that could be enjoyed, shared, and revisited time and again. In spring 2013, a year after we launched Beyond the Flavor, we began conceptualizing that publication. We wanted to create something that would reflect the rich, collaborative, supportive network we had uncovered. So we created a sponsorship model in which businesses or individuals could sponsor stories about another person or business working in our local food community, one they felt had a story to tell. We approached a collection of folks we'd met, and were profoundly grateful when a dozen of them signed on to this first edition of *Commons*. It was a tremendous leap of faith, and we feel fortunate that they placed their trust in us.

We embarked on telling the stories our sponsors chose, taking the same collaborative approach we so admire in our local food community. In addition to our portraits and images, we enlisted the skills of a local writer to tell these stories in rich, descriptive language fitting of our subjects. A local artist helped us craft maps that capture the beauty of this region's geography, and other local writers sent in essays describing their connection with food in Charlottesville. A skilled designer helped us craft a layout and aesthetic befitting of this project. As a finishing touch, we asked local food enthusiasts, producers, bakers, and chefs to share a food-related memory of their town. Combined, these talents produced the publication you now hold.

This edition of *Commons* explores the interplay between place and food through the lenses of history, tradition, and innovation. We hope the stories shared within these pages deepen your appreciation for the food culture of this beautiful place we call home.

Warmly,
Andrea + Sarah

OUR TEAM

ANDREA HUBBELL specializes in interior, lifestyle, and culinary photography. With a background and education in architectural design, Andrea has cultivated an appreciation for form, space, composition and color that is present in every image she creates. In 2008, the launch of her recipe blog, Bella Eats, sparked a passion for food photography and led to the creation of Andrea Hubbell Photography in 2010.

Sharing food is a way of sharing love, and some of the best moments of Andrea's life have been spent around a table with her favorite people, eating and listening to their stories. When not behind the camera or in the kitchen, Andrea enjoys collaborating with her husband, Brian, on design and house projects and loving on their two labrador retrievers. She anxiously awaits the arrival of her first son in autumn 2013.

SARAH CRAMER SHIELDS specializes in environmental portraiture and documenting her subjects with honest, accurate images. Dual degrees in Fine Art Photography and Anthropology serve as a natural extension of her desire to understand others and make beautiful images. Sarah has documented people professionally since 2005 through her studio, Cramer Photo. She lives to tell stories with her photographs.

Sarah spends her days documenting people, creating in the kitchen, working on an old house, and living life well with her husband, Matt, and their two dogs, Charley and Crosby. She is overjoyed with the anticipated arrival of her first son in August 2013.

JENNY PAURYS is a professional writer and editor with a background in creative nonfiction and news writing. As owner of Fine Lines Editing, she helps a wide range of clients produce concise, polished text for projects large and small. An interest in sustainable living led her to this project, because she feels the choices we make about the food we consume present us with a tangible opportunity to have a meaningful, positive impact on our community, country, and planet.

Jenny lives in the Belmont neighborhood of Charlottesville, where she and her husband, Egidijus, are raising three sweet children who like to chase chickens, climb trees, and eat strawberries straight from the garden.

GET IN TOUCH
beyondtheflavor.com

ACKNOWLEDGMENTS

As with the food community we have come to know since we
embarked on this project, this publication owes its existence
to the efforts of many. We are especially grateful for the support
of our husbands, families and friends, who have listened
to our endless discussions, offered their opinions and ideas,
and lent their support wherever it was needed.

We extend our sincere gratitude to the following individuals and
businesses, who were part of the creation of this publication:

MATT THOMAS, CONVOY
Design + Layout
weareconvoy.com

DANI ANTOL, ROCK PAPER SCISSORS
Hand-Drawn Maps
thinkrockpaperscissors.com

COMMONS SPONSORS
Without whom this publication wouldn't have been possible.
Learn more about them on pages 150–151.

SPECIAL THANKS TO
Bliss Abbot, Polina Oganesyan + Erin Kennedy
And, of course, Jeff Cornejo, who introduced us.

IMAGES BY Andrea Hubbell + Sarah Cramer Shields.
WORDS BY Jenny Paurys, except where otherwise noted and *The Family Picnic*, which had multiple authors.

TABLE *of* CONTENTS

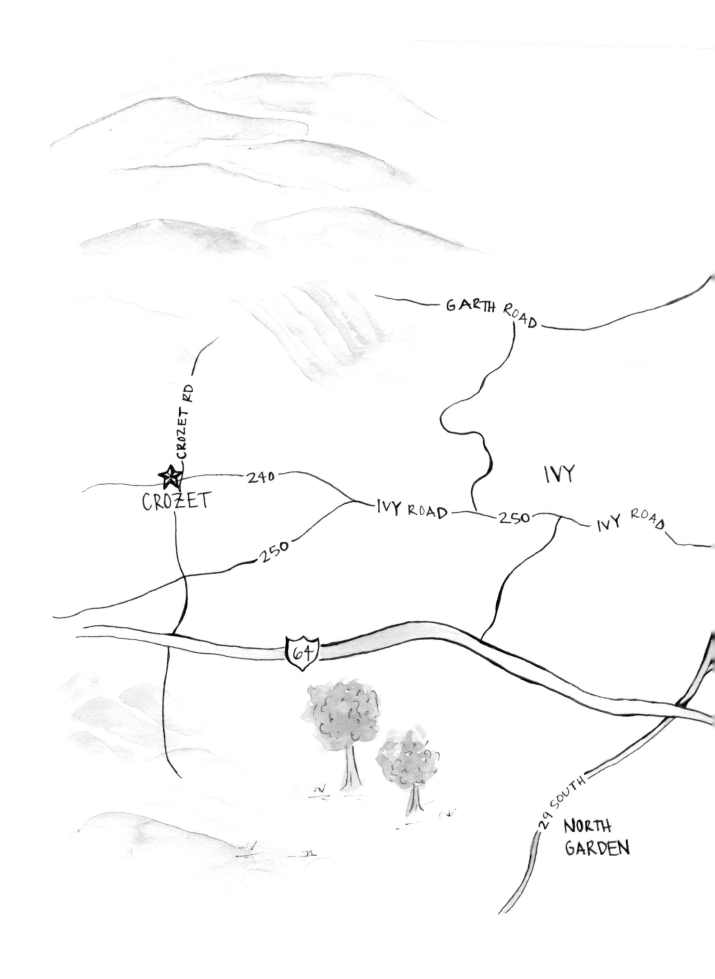

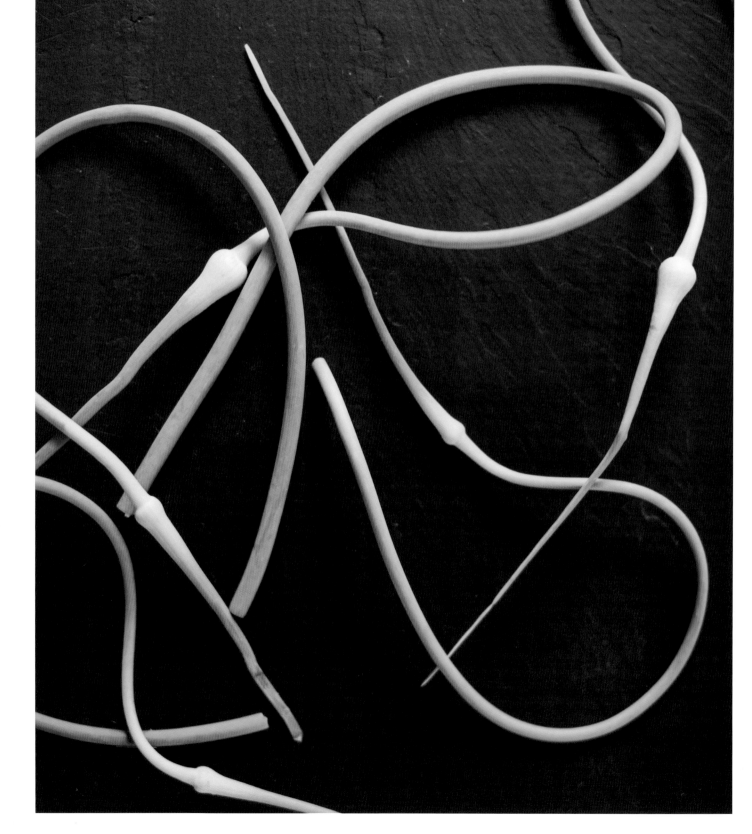

GARLIC SCAPES

Charred Garlic Scapes Vinaigrette

Tucker Yoder | Clifton Inn

INGREDIENTS

1 bunch garlic scapes
⅓ c malt vinegar
½ c canola oil
½ c extra virgin olive oil
1 T dijon mustard
salt and pepper, to taste

DIRECTIONS

Char half the garlic scapes in a cast iron pan on one side until black. Remove and let cool.

Blanch remaining scapes in large pot of salted water; shock in ice water.

Rough chop all scapes. Blend mustard, vinegar, and scapes in food processor; continue to blend and drizzle in both oils in a steady stream. The result will be a chunky vinaigrette.

Season to taste with salt and pepper. Use as a dressing for fish, pasta, beef or salad.

Pickled Garlic Scapes

Angelo Vangelopoulos | Ivy Inn

INGREDIENTS

1 lb garlic scapes, washed, patted dry, cut into approx.
    3-inch lengths (so they'll fit into your jars)
2 c red wine vinegar
2 c water
3 T salt
2 t sugar
1 t yellow mustard seed
1 t whole black pepper
1 t allspice
1 bay leaf
3 cloves
½ inch piece of ginger, peeled

DIRECTIONS

Put the vinegar, water, salt, sugar and spices in a medium-sized nonreactive pot and bring to a boil.

Add the scapes, and return to a boil. Cover and let stand 30 minutes.

Transfer scapes and the pickling brine into a clean, nonreactive container and store under refrigeration, or put in canning jars and follow manufacturer's instructions for canning and preserving.

A great compliment to cured meats and hard cheeses.

Charlottesville's Edible Classrooms

Schoolyards across Charlottesville are teeming with activity, but not just the usual kind found in playgrounds and rec fields. Rather than shouts and cheers, it is the din of bees and birds and the pulse of leaves and blooms, as former fields and unused corners give way to classrooms of a different sort: gardens.

Started at Buford Middle School in spring 2010, the City Schoolyard Garden project was up and running at all six elementary schools in the Charlottesville city school system by spring 2013. This effort has required inspiration and dedication, and it found its champion in Linda Winecoff, mother of two graduates of Charlottesville City Schools, who was captivated by a 2004 article in *The New York Times* about Alice Waters, founder and chef of Chez Panisse in Berkeley, California, and her efforts to cultivate a garden at a middle school in Berkeley. Linda felt confident that Charlottesville, with its small, vibrant school system, was the ideal place to try something similar.

With a background in landscape architecture and a passion for gardening, Linda felt equipped to advocate for such a program. But she, in turn, needed a champion. She found it in Eric Johnson, principal at Buford Middle School. When she and a group of friends supportive of the initiative approached him in autumn 2009, he instantly got on board. With a background in counseling, he saw how the garden could serve as a place of reflection. He told her if she could find funding and devise a plan to care for the gardens that did not place a burden on the teachers at his school, he would give them a place to grow.

So Linda did something she'd never done before: she and a couple other supporters of the project wrote a grant. To her delight, it was selected by the Prana Fund, a charitable investment vehicle managed by the Charlottesville Area Community Foundation. The project was awarded the funds necessary to create the garden at Buford and establish the infrastructure to manage the initiative, including a board to oversee the project and a part-time garden educator, Rachel Williamson. They picked a site for the garden near the school, and designed its layout in Linda's kitchen one afternoon that winter. In April 2010, volunteers from the community helped put in

> *"Wayne couldn't really believe that the tiny dots we were planting in the garden back in February would become a plant. Now, he rips the leaves from the plant and eats them right there in the garden, and tells me how much he loves spinach— his teeth turning green in the process."*

Matt Darring

Garden Coordinator, Burnley-Moran Elementary School

the beds. A local construction company donated materials for a fence, and the Buford Middle School garden was born.

Two years passed. Thanks to the efforts of two garden educators—first Rachel, and then Emily Axelbaum—teachers, parents, and students became engaged in the project, seeing how it could benefit the student body by providing an outdoor classroom where students could learn about the science of plants, the process of growing food, the interaction of natural systems, and have a place to reflect and unwind. In 2012, Dr. Rosa Atkins, superintendent of Charlottesville City Schools, asked City Schoolyard Garden to expand the initiative to all six elementary schools, offering a modest amount of funding to allow this transformation to take place. In tandem with this, the board hired an executive director, Jeanette Abi-Nader, the parent of a Greenbrier Elementary student who had previously been a volunteer with the program and brought with her a rich background in small- and large-scale farming. Linda, in turn, became the program director, overseeing the ef-

forts of the part-time garden coordinators at each school—parents paid a small stipend for their time—who ensure that the gardens are tended and cared for, freeing up teachers to utilize the gardens for educational purposes. Throughout the 2012–2013 school year, gardens were created at each of the city's elementary schools, each as unique in its structure and layout as the schools themselves.

Linda's instinct that Charlottesville was the ideal place for such a program turned out to be the case. With the City Schoolyard Garden program taking root across the city, the initiative now must look to the future and to finding sustaining donors that can help the program continue to develop and serve the children of our community.

"Gardening is not something that you can sit down and learn at a computer," Linda points out. "It is literally a hands-on, mentoring relationship. And you have to be together, shoulder to shoulder. It's that kind of relationship. The more staff we have, the more volunteers we have, the more that magic connection will take place." ◆

LENI COVINGTON, A PREKINDERGARTEN TEACHER AT BURLEY-MORAN ELEMENTARY, OFTEN TAKES GROUPS OF HER STUDENTS OUT TO THE GARDEN TO SING TO THE PLANTS. THESE ARE A FEW OF THEIR FAVORITE SONGS.

In the springtime garden,
rosy morning glow,
Earth is waiting, waiting, waiting,
for the seeds to grow.

◆ ◆ ◆

Spring is coming, spring is coming. Flowers are coming, too.
Pansies, lilies, daffodillies—all are coming through.
Spring is coming, spring is coming. Birdies, build your nest.
Weave together, straw and feather—each one doing your best.
Spring is coming, spring is coming. All around is fair.
Shimmer, glimmer, on the river—joy is everywhere.

◆ ◆ ◆

Strawberries, wake up! Spring is coming, spring is coming.
Strawberries, wake up! Spring is coming, spring is near.

The Rising Tide

Gail Hobbs-Page has big plans for Virginia cheese. On her twenty-five-acre Caromont Farm in Esmont, Virginia, southwest of Charlottesville, Gail tends to a herd of nearly 100 goats—including le manchas, saanens, alpines, and toggenburgs—and creates a half-dozen varieties of goat's and cow's milk cheeses that have gained a devoted following in Virginia and beyond.

Gail started making cheese in 2007 after a decades-long career as a chef. She says that she started out with some naive and romantic notions of what it would be like to run a creamery—notions she quickly lost when the reality of running a farm as a business settled in. "We've had some very, very good luck, and we've also learned from our mistakes," Gail says, reflecting on the journey she's taken with Caromont. "What we've tried to do is take ourselves seriously. Take our cheeses seriously, and really put everything we have into making them better."

For Gail, this has meant investing in the future with new vats, presses and milking systems, as well as traveling to other artisan cheese producers to learn new methods and approaches. Beyond all the infrastructure to improve craft and technique, one of the biggest investments Gail is making is training others. One of her success stories in that department is Na-

than Vergin, who came to her by way of her friends Joel and Teresa Salatin and Polyface Farm in Staunton, Virginia. She called the Salatins up during her second year running the creamery, wondering if they had any interns they could recommend. As a matter of fact, they did.

"We felt like we were the interns, he worked us so hard," she says with a laugh, reflecting the energy Nathan brought to his time at Caromont. "Nathan reminds me of an old-fashioned farmer, the kind that I haven't seen in a long time. He just works, all the time."

Nathan dreamed of his own farm, and Gail felt strongly that he had much to bring to Central Virginia's food community. She did what she could to support his search for a farm to call his own, something he eventually found at the old dairy in Nelson County, south of Charlottesville. The farm was very run-down, but Nathan saw its potential.

"I went to that farm with Nathan and I looked around and I thought, 'Oh Lord—he's got his work cut out for him.' But you know what he said? He said, 'This place is going to be great. I have everything I need here. My cows will have everything they need here. And he's cleaned up that place; his milk house is gorgeous. I'm so proud of him," she says.

> *"We have to stick together. We have to market ourselves and be a unified food region. That's how we get somewhere."*

The farm operation Nathan built at that old dairy is now known as Silky Cow, and one of its customers is Gail. With Silky Cow milk, Gail creates cheeses like local favorite Bloomsbury, crafted from pasteurized cow's milk with a bloomy rind, made in the style of a chaource.

For Gail, this kind of mentorship is key to putting Virginia cheese on the map. "We already have more cheesemakers coming to Virginia as a result of Caromont," she says. "It makes me proud. You mentor your competition, but that's what we have to have in order to rise. The rising tide floats all boats."

And indeed, this very tide is what Gail sees as the way forward for Virginia cheesemakers. She points out that to get there, cheesemakers need support from other Virginia food industries, like wineries, as well as favorable legislation that allows small farmers the opportunity to put down roots in the state.

"That's how we have to do it," she says. "We have to stick together. We have to market ourselves and be a unified food region. That's how we get somewhere."

From her booth at the Farmers in the Park market at Meade Park, Gail looks in her element, selling her handcrafted cheeses to new and repeat customers alike. "Our love is *local*," she says. "We love selling at farmers' markets. We love selling at small specialty stores where we can have a relationship."

"One of the things I see that pleases me so much is everyone in this community has ownership of Caromont," she adds. "They're proud when they take it to other places, and they can say, 'This is *our* cheese.' That is the whole idea—that's how we develop this area as a food region." ◆

The Quarter-Acre CSA

THIS STORY IS SPONSORED BY

JM Stock Provisions & Supply

Down a country road in Keswick, Virginia, in a meadow near an old red barn, there is a large garden with a dozen long rows bursting with life. Large, leafy squash plants sport bright yellow blooms; rambling melon vines cascade over the edge of a mounded row; cucumber plants crest the top of old wooden fence trellises; spring green lettuce heads and dark green leafy beets stand tall and ready for harvest. The 8,000-square-foot plot is surrounded by a tall fence made of slender metal posts and flexible netted fencing, with a gate fashioned out of two old doors. Before the garden was here, this space was just a meadow. That was before David Rogers moved in.

In autumn 2012, David got to thinking about a garden. A native of Winchester, he had recently returned to Virginia after living in Vermont for a spell, taking up residence in a small farmhouse on this 125-acre farm, and the expansive fields surrounding him seemed ripe for a proper garden. But as he considered where to put it and what to grow, that idea evolved into something bigger—a way to share the bounty he envisioned with others. Rather than a personal garden, he could create a CSA.

Community-supported agriculture, or CSA, is a structure under which a group of people pool resources to support the production of food by a particular farm or grower. Each person pays a lump sum for a "share," which entitles them to a set amount of the food, typically on a weekly basis throughout the growing season. During his time in Vermont, David had volunteered on farms and had been surrounded by a community of enthusiastic gardeners, small farmers, and CSAs of all sizes.

"I saw different ways people do it: big CSAs with over two hundred people, smaller ones," he says, reflecting on that experience. "I started to think of the spectrum that exists between 200-plus share market farmers and the backyard gardener. And I realized—it doesn't have to look a certain way. There are different ways that growing food can fit into a community."

David started researching how much food to grow and harvest per share. He created a detailed spreadsheet, taking into account the space each plant would need to help him determine the proper size of the garden. The original plan called for a half-acre plot, but he realized that with proper planting, he could scale it back to a more manageable size—eighty by 100 feet. David determined that the garden could support five CSA shares, with each member receiving vegetables once a week for twenty weeks, along with one broiler chicken over the course of the season. He emailed some friends to see if anyone was interested.

Among those who received this email were James Lum and Matthew Greene, owners of local butcher shop JM Stock Provisions, and both Winchester natives who grew up with David. They welcomed the idea of this small-scale CSA because as James and Matthew see it, local food production is vital to the long-term viability of a community.

"I think it's very important for folks not only to know where their food comes from, but also to have a relationship with the person or persons responsible for producing it," says Matthew. Projects like David's allow for this connection.

David suggests that this relationship between grower and consumer is a natural partnership. Harkening back to his childhood in Winchester, he notes how his family was one of a group of about eight that regularly gathered for socializing, barbecues, church events, and the like. Just as common values and lifestyles drew those individuals together, he sees an opportunity for small-scale agriculture to do the same.

"What I am trying to create is a system or model that small communities can adopt that will provide them with good health, experiential education, and a belief system rooted in food values around which to unite and identify, together," he says.

David had hoped Charlottesville was the right kind of community for his vision of a small-scale CSA, and it turns out he was right: the five shares sold in a week's time. Feeling the full reality of the project, he quickly ordered seeds and started them under grow lights in the farmhouse. When the ground warmed up, he began clearing the garden plot. He used a tractor to clear-cut the pasture, borrowed a friend's tiller to break up the soil, and then went back with a hoe to shape and define the rows. He did all of this by himself, and mentions almost as an afterthought that he did it while holding down a full-time job at local online grocer Relay Foods. When you ask him how on earth he managed it, his response is humble and matter-of-fact. He just did.

The feeling you get when you talk with David is that he jumped into this project with both feet and never looked back. As he walks among the rows of thriving plants, his genuine enthusiasm for this project is contagious. And it is this quality of David's undertaking that stands out for James, who at

"He embodies the hope and idea that anyone can create a part for themselves, and there's always room for one more."

one point toyed with the idea of becoming a farmer, but felt the barrier to entry too great.

"I feel like David represents something that's pretty unique about Charlottesville and about our generation, because he just did it," James says. "I think a lot of people—like me—don't do it, because they think they need a financial backer or hundreds of thousands of dollars and all this land to do anything of worth, but it's not true."

The inspiration James sees in David's decision to embark on this project is something he hopes can be cultivated in more people. "He embodies the hope and idea that anyone can create a part for themselves, and there's always room for one more," he says. James points out that each person can strive for more direct involvement in the food system, and there are many ways to find that involvement, be it preparing a meal for yourself or growing your own food. "It doesn't really matter what you're in it for," he adds, "it just matters that you're in it."

Standing in the garden, marveling at his friend's accomplishment, James reflects on the community that attracts folks like David and himself, and fosters projects like this quarter-acre CSA.

"David said something the other day that really stuck in my head," James says, gazing out over the garden. "He said that there are many different interpretations of local food in Charlottesville. I like that."

We do, too. ◆

A Local Affair

THIS STORY IS SPONSORED BY

Amore Events by Cody, LLC

Charlottesville locals know that the best time to go to the City Market on Saturday is *early*, while the bins of fruits and vegetables are overflowing, the sun is low in the sky, and most of the city is still asleep. Gay Beery knows this secret. Owner of A Pimento Catering, and a Charlottesville-area resident for more than 20 years, Gay is at the market almost every Saturday morning throughout the season, getting in touch with what's growing, gathering supplies for the coming week, and checking in with vendors and friends.

This particular morning starts out relatively cool for a late spring day. As we walk among the stalls, it is clear that Gay knows nearly all the vendors here. She is unhurried, chatting with each one. Her demeanor is relaxed and collected, and she shows a genuine interest in every person she engages in conversation. All the while, she is collecting ingredients she will need for two events in the coming days: a bridal lunch that will take place later that day and a tasting of simple summer hors d'oeuvres she will hold for us.

At that tasting a few days later, Gay is back in A Pimento's simple kitchen when we arrive, blending a chilled soup featuring spring onions picked up at the City Market, sweet peas, fava beans, mint, coriander, ginger, a touch of buttermilk, and a dusting of ground sumac. She spoons the savory soup into simple, vintage green glass cups. Its flavor is equal parts bright and earthy and wholly refreshing, with the bean and pea in the puree offering a complex texture and the buttermilk lending a lovely tang.

When she first moved to Charlottesville in the early 1990s from the Washington, D.C., area, Gay found her comfort zone at the City Market. "The farmers' market is what I really clicked with," she says. "It was so easy just to go and get the freshest possible produce. Nobody used the word local back then—it was just common sense."

The fact that Gay takes time for this touchstone each Saturday morning is especially remarkable given the volume of weddings A Pimento caters in a given year—a number that will crest forty in 2013. Charlottesville has become one of the most popular wedding destinations in the country, and those supporting this industry are racing to keep up with demand. Gay says that though the work can be exhausting, the variety of clients she meets provides ample opportunity for creativity. Cody Grannis, who has joined us for this afternoon tasting, agrees. Cody became familiar with Gay and A Pimento while serving as an event planner for the University of Virginia. Now a wedding planner, Cody's business, Amore Events, will help more than sixty couples design weddings in Charlottesville this year; Cody herself will have a wedding every weekend from spring through fall. Her advice to brides is to choose talented professionals to assist with the various components of their wedding, and then let those

professionals do what they do best. Cody feels A Pimento is among the finest catering operations in Charlottesville.

"They take so much care and pride in the way that their food looks and the way that it tastes," she says. "I love that when we meet with Gay for a consultation and she talks with my clients about the food and local ingredients, she really knows what she's talking about. It impresses my clients." For Gay, one of the benefits of the wedding industry growing in Charlottesville has been the opportunity to work with wedding planners more often. Gay feels the organization someone like Cody lends to the process allows her work to shine.

For this afternoon's tasting, Gay has prepared something she makes frequently for clients: pizza. The soft, thin wheat crust is topped with items she gathered at the City Market on Saturday—roasted mushrooms from North Cove, Bloomsbury cheese from Caromont Farm, savory and thyme, as well as pheasant confit sourced from local private estate Highbrighton Farm. Gay lays the pizza out on a long wooden board and we stand in A Pimento's front room around a wooden farm table with a seagreen patina, devouring the slices. The combination of the confit, mushrooms, and cheese is rich, pleasantly salty, chewy, and satisfying. For a beverage, Gay's assistant, Brooke Ray, mixes another A Pimento favorite, a smoked ginger and lime syrup mixed with sparkling water, served over ice.

Back in the kitchen, we watch Gay skillfully assemble two other hors d'oeuvres, both populated with items from her recent City Market haul. The first features crostini decked with goat milk feta from Caromont Farm, a wedge of roasted golden beet, drizzled saba—a reduction of unfermented grape juice—and slices of nasturtium seed, which adds a zesty flavor to the creamy cheese and subtly sweet beet.

For the second, on another type of crostini, she adds a layer of paté made at A Pimento from Free Union Grass Farm chicken liver—also picked up at the market—with rhubarb-cherry chutney spooned over top, garnished with green garlic. Gay tries to source as many of her ingredients as locally as she can, something made more possible with the increase in small farmers and food artisans amid the local food revolution.

"I've been sourcing from local people for a long time, but it's gotten easier as it's gotten more accepted," she says. "Farmers have more work and they're able to transport more, produce more, and know that they can sell it. It's been a great sea change."

The two hors d'oeuvres are laid out on a simple antique wooden tray atop fig leaves plucked from a tree outside, and we go back for seconds and then thirds, enjoying the crunch of the crostini, and the mix of savory and sweet on each. The light has started to take on the golden hue of a summer afternoon. We sit around the room, the conversation meandering, with a genuine easiness inspired by Gay's comfortable presence, feeling as though we have stolen an hour of serenity amid a hectic summer. We all linger there, savoring it. ◆

RECIPES ON PAGE 144

CHARLOTTESVILLE & ITS FOODWAYS

Mark Gresge | Chef + Owner, l'étoile Restaurant

I am inspired by our town's history. I am amazed at the generations of families that have lived here for over a hundred years. I embrace the local traditions and admire the locals' knowledge. Of course, I'll never be a local no matter how long I live here, and I respect that.

I really love the sense of community, the common goals of promoting our culinary history. It's comforting to me. I am very committed to my small town and I feel small acts are appreciated. I want to step up to the plate and be a good neighbor and friend. I strive to be an asset to my wonderful small town. As a chef, food and its preparation can help with that idea. But how to go about it?

The advice I like to give young chefs, or really anybody who'll listen to me, is not to wait around for inspiration. Inspiration is for amateurs; the rest of us just show up and get to work. If you wait around for the clouds to part and a bolt of lightning to strike you in the brain, you are not going to make an awful lot of work. All the best ideas come out of the process; they come out of the work itself. Things occur to you. If you're sitting around trying to dream up a great idea about food, you can sit there a long time before anything happens. But if you just get to work, something will occur to you and something else will occur to you and something else that you reject will push you in another direction. Inspiration is absolutely unnecessary and somehow deceptive. You feel like you need this great idea before you can get down to work, and I find that's almost never the case. Get started and set a course for yourself.

Perhaps plant a garden. Or visit the farmers' market and see what our neighbors are growing. Try and prepare food at home. Or dine in one of many of the restau-

> ## "Inspiration is for amateurs; the rest of us just show up and get to work."

rants in town that are actively participating in our wonderful heritage. The local food movement may be just the ticket to save food traditions and plant varieties that are on the brink of becoming a museum piece. As people shift their focus back to their specific region and place, they rediscover the foods that grow specifically and sometimes exclusively in that particular area—foods that their predecessors knew well. Recovering food sources goes hand in hand with recovering food traditions: old methods of growing foods, recipes, folklore, festivals, and other ways to honor local, whole food and culture. ◆

FAMILY FORAGE

Tucker Yoder | Executive Chef, Clifton Inn

A cool late summer or early fall morning with the mist just lifting into the Blue Ridge and the drops of the last few days of rain still dripping from the trees: this is one of the favorite times for the Yoder family. It is days like this that gets kids get out of bed early and Mom and Dad out of the house before the first cup of tea. We all know that out there waiting for us is the beautiful orange mushroom we all love so much—the chanterelle. Right in our backyard we have found pounds of them over the last three years, and they continue to sprout up in new places and new times of the season, keeping us on our toes.

Chanterelles are a great mushroom for kids to find because the are such a unique color against the surrounding forest floor that they can be seen from fifty yards away in some cases. Generally when you find one, there are a couple dozen more nearby. Once we have filled our bags with these fragrant little fungi, we rush back the the house for chanterelle omelettes with a bit of Appalachian cheese. ◆

One Farm, Five Chefs

THIS STORY IS SPONSORED BY

Timbercreek Organics

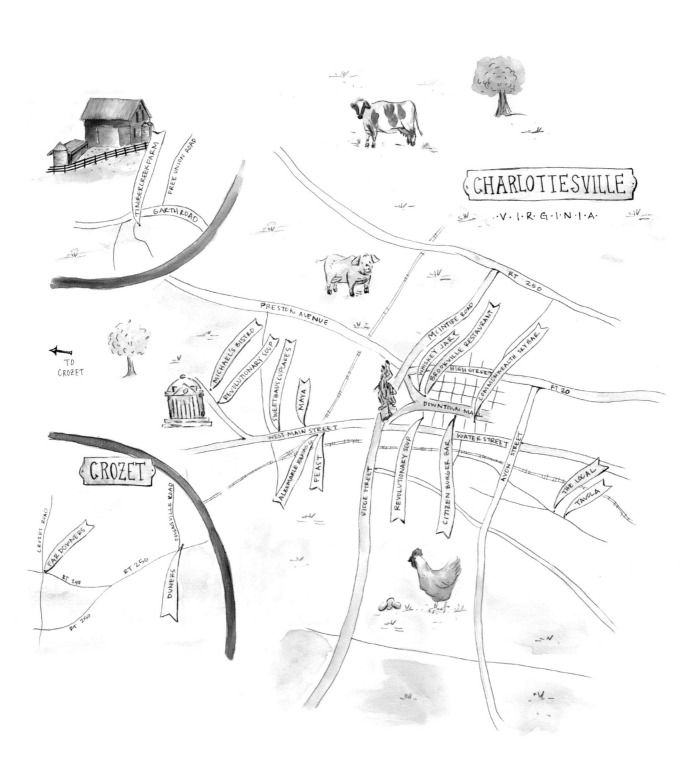

Looking out the door of the old red barn at Timbercreek Farm on an early summer afternoon, what greets the eye is as close to the idyllic picture of Virginia countryside as it gets: green fields capping hill after hill as far as one can see, ribbons of forest running through the valleys, and fields divided by clean, sturdy fences that blend into the landscape. In the distance, cows graze in a pasture—dots on a lush green hillside against a backdrop of blue sky.

Closer to the barn, a handful of chickens meander on the edge of the gravel road surrounding the building. This land—located just five miles from Barrack's Road Shopping Center—has been in Zach Miller's family since the 1970s, and was a horse farm

hundred cows, two hundred pigs, and five hundred ducks, as well as staple vegetables, including lettuce, spinach, tomatoes, cucumbers and peppers, among others.

While they have accomplished an impressive amount in a short time, it has all been approached with a distinct mindfulness. Zach, who good-naturedly calls himself "the brawn of this operation" emphasizes that the farm he and Sara are building on these 500 acres is a complete system. The animals they have chosen to raise complement one another and are able to share the land in rotation, each playing a distinct role, and none overtaxing it. They grow food their customers want to consume, and they only add things the system can support.

"The most important component has been developing relationships we can count on."

for several decades. When Zach and his wife, Sara, came to live here and assumed management of it in 2006, it was far from picturesque. The pastures needed reseeding; the fences needed repair. Much energy was spent in the initial years on improving and creating the infrastructure to support the farm the Millers envisioned. During that time, they slowly ramped up the farm's production, beginning with 2,000 chickens raised for meat, five hundred egg-laying hens, fifty cows, fifty pigs, and a hundred turkeys. Each year they increased their herds and flocks. In 2013, their fourth year as a production farm, the Millers and their small crew of farm assistants will raise and process eight thousand chickens for meat, another thousand for eggs, more than a

Sara and Zach are both quick to say that the key to their farm's success has been their extensive relationships with commercial clients in the Charlottesville area, including restaurants and bakeries. They have spent the past several years developing those relationships, and are quick to point out that without those clients, they would not have seen this level of success in such a short amount of time.

"The most important component has been developing relationships we can count on, so when we put pigs in the pasture, we know we are going to be able to sell those pigs," Zach says. "That's not something we can do if we haven't developed relationships with the chefs to know the demand will be there."

"We as chefs are nothing without our farmers, who most importantly are our neighbors and friends."

BROOKVILLE

Harrison Keevil

One of these chefs is Harrison Keevil of Brookville Restaurant, located at the far end of the Downtown Mall. Harrison and his wife, Jennifer, opened the 60-seat restaurant in the summer of 2010. There, Harrison cooks up what he calls "New American cuisine," with a menu that changes often, inspired by what is new and fresh. The Keevils' mission when they launched Brookville was to source as much locally as possible, and they have stood by that goal, with an impressive 95% of their ingredients sourced locally year-round.

Brookville's eggs, ducks, chickens, beef and pork all come exclusively from Timbercreek. While that may seem like a lot of eggs in one basket, so to speak, Harrison is genuine in his enthusiasm for the farm. "I believe flat out that they raise the best chickens, pigs and cattle, so that is why we use them," Harrison says, matter-of-factly. "I believe the farm itself creates a special flavor in these animals that is unique to Timbercreek. Their stuff just tastes better; it tastes real."

RECIPE ON PAGE 145

ALBEMARLE BAKING CO.

Gerry Newman

Restaurants aren't the only dedicated Timbercreek customers. Over in the Main Street Market, Albemarle Baking Company owner Gerry Newman sources all of his eggs from the farm. "Every decision regarding ingredients is made with the customer in mind," he says. "Quality, flavor, and value are the guidelines in the choices we make. In the case of the eggs we use from Timbercreek, I can go to the farm and see how the hens live; I can crack open an egg and see the great color of the yolk. I can talk to the farmer and his wife; walk through the fields with them and their children. Zach and Sara are lovely and the care they take in their product shows in our baked goods."

Albemarle Baking Co. opened in 1995. Since then, Gerry has seen an evolution in Charlottesville's food scene. "It is amazing how things have changed in our area in the 18 years since we first opened Albemarle Baking Co.," he says. "There are wonderful places to eat in neighborhoods all over town. People rave about the food community in Portland, Oregon, (my hometown), but we have plenty to be proud of right here in central Virginia."

RECIPE ON PAGE 145

"Our goal is to offer the best-possible bread, pastries, and cakes to our customers. Using organic, local ingredients helps us meet that goal every day."

"*My goals as far as local ingredients are simple. I want to fill the menu with more and more great local ingredients. The higher percentage of ingredients that are local, the better.*"

THE LOCAL

Matthew Hart

Across the bridge from downtown Charlottesville, in the Belmont neighborhood, Chef Matthew Hart at The Local is also emphatic in his appreciation for the quality of meat Timbercreek is producing. "I think that Timbercreek has about the perfect chicken," he says, noting that while the menu can vary greatly at The Local, the chicken is a constant. "The chickens we get from Timbercreek have the perfect balance of flavor and plumpness. The birds are meaty and full of flavor, which is about all you can ask of a humble chicken."

Since opening in early 2008, The Local has become a pillar of the increasingly popular downtown Belmont restaurant scene, and local ingredients are the restaurant's focus. "I would still say that the main reason that I use local ingredients is because I want to put the best possible dish I can on my customers' plate, and using as many locally sourced ingredients as possible is, in general, the best way to accomplish that goal," Matthew explains. "That said, once you open your eyes to sustainable, local food production as well as some of the practices of large-scale commercial food production, there is no way to close your eyes and go back to the old way of doing things."

 RECIPE ON PAGE 145

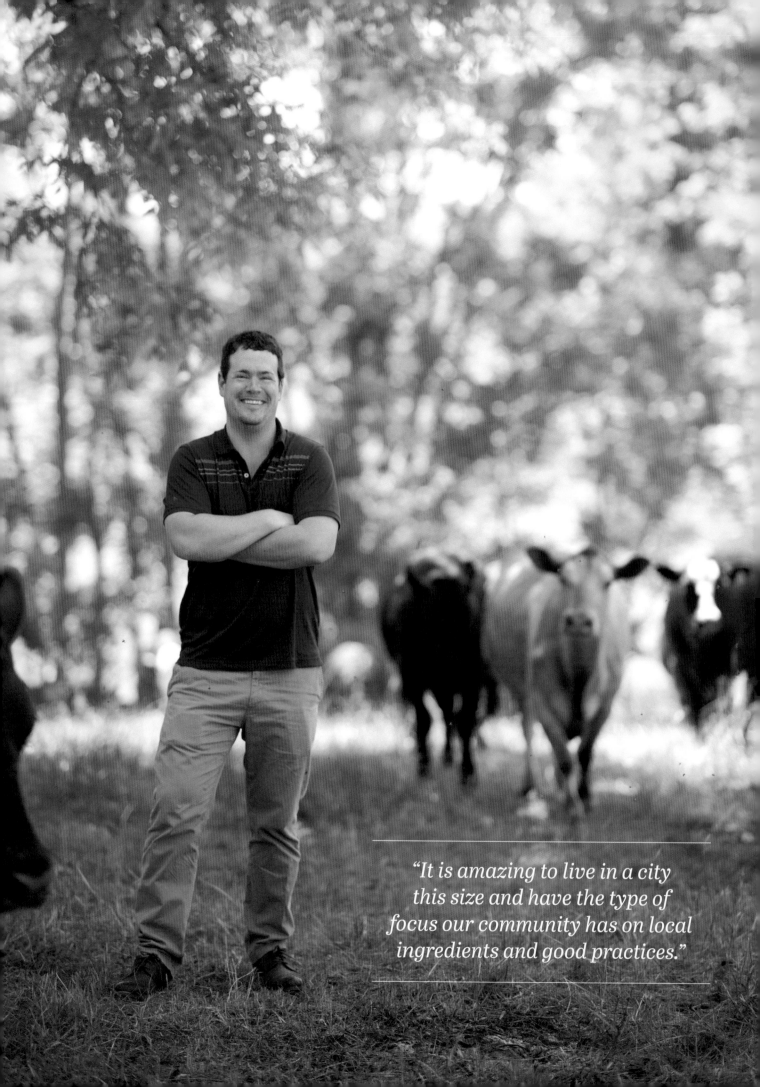

"It is amazing to live in a city this size and have the type of focus our community has on local ingredients and good practices."

CITIZEN BURGER BAR

Andy McClure

Located squarely in the center of the Downtown Mall is another Timbercreek commercial client: Citizen Burger Bar. Proprietor Anderson McClure owns several other Charlottesville flagship eateries, including The Virginian Restaurant, West Main Restaurant, Three Restaurant, and The Biltmore Grill. When it comes to Citizen Burger, Andy tries to source as many items locally as he can. But most importantly, he feels the main ingredient of the eatery—its beef—has to come from a local source.

"Our use of Timbercreek products was the result of extensive research about cattle farms both in the area and nationally," Andy says. "We wanted a local farm, but more importantly, we wanted a farm that had fantastic practices. We wanted someone that was better than the competition. It was pretty amazing to find such a fantastic operation right in our backyard."

Andy is devoted to the concept of grass-fed beef—only half-jokingly claiming, "Grass-fed beef will save the world!" Noting that grass-fed beef has more nutrients, is lower in calories, and comes with fewer health risk factors, he also points out that grass is the natural diet of cows. Timbercreek's focus on this natural diet, plus their commitment to not using hormones or antibiotics, is key for Andy.

"They treat the animals properly, and free grazing on rotated grassland is as normal and natural as it gets," he says. "We're talking happy grass-fed cows here!"

RECIPE ON PAGE 146

"The cultural and economical impact supporting local food can have on a community present a holistic wellness for the society as well as the individual."

REVOLUTIONARY SOUP + THE WHISKEY JAR

Will Richey

Further west on the Downtown Mall and down a side street, Revolutionary Soup also uses Timbercreek products. Purchased by Chef Will Richey in 2005, this favorite lunch spot offers scores of homemade soups each day, as well as a host of sandwiches and wraps. In early 2012, Will opened The Whiskey Jar at the far end of the Downtown Mall, specializing in traditional Virginia fare.

Will sources as much as 70% of the food at both restaurants locally. "We are always trying to use more," he says, "but we are proud of the amount we have achieved in our low-cost, high-volume establishments."

As one might imagine, traditional Virginian cooking includes a lot of meat. Each week, Will receives a whole pig from Timbercreek, which he uses for pork chops, barbecue, bacon, ribs, and tenderloin. He also gets two cases of eggs from the farm every week and almost 70 chickens, which turn up on his menus in the form of fried chicken, sandwiches, soups, barbecue chicken, and many types of specials, like pork belly sandwich. In the winter, Will buys a whole cow about every three weeks.

"Timbercreek is unwavering in their dedication to holistic animal management," Will says. "Their knowledge and dedication is continually evident in the quality of their product and if you want the best in sustainability, flavor and quality, there is no other choice in this area." ◆

RECIPE ON PAGE 146

EMPTY NESTERS

Sheila Cervelloni | Owner, The Bakery Box

It was a late August afternoon—our first weekend as empty nesters. It was the first of many Saturdays where Tom and I had to sell doughnuts at the City Market without the help of our children. We got hit, and hit hard. There was no worrying about arguments, who was doing what, or whose turn it was to scrape out the doughnut hopper. We put our heads down and got to work. We knew what needed to be done.

Most Saturdays we want to end the exhausting day with several beers, but today was different. It was peaceful, calm. The sun was out, the humidity was gone, and a light, cooling breeze occasionally brushed through. The constant worrying about our children was gone—for the moment. We realized we had all afternoon to ourselves. After twenty-two years of struggling to have a date, we held each other's hands and walked to the Downtown Mall. We needed lunch and decided on Petit Pois, a quaint French café and bistro with patio seating. Wine was a must. Tom always orders and he chose a white. As usual, we started off with a cheese plate, but also ordered the chicken liver mousse as a special treat. Now, you might be thinking, how is chicken liver ever any kind of treat? Well, if you have it at Petit Pois, then you will know. It is light, creamy and the flavor is just amazing. I think I even divided up the plate so that we would each get our own fair share.

Next was our entrée. I had the gnocchi Parisians with fresh carrot puree and peas and mushrooms. The gnocchis were light and tender, yet firm enough to scoop up the garnish. But I think what put the dish over the top was the carrot purée. It was sweet, light and tasted so fresh. You would have thought that the peas were spring peas—young, tender, and sweet. The whole dish tasted like they had pulled the ingredients out of their garden that morning. It was fresh and alive.

I remember pausing for a brief moment, gazing at my husband, thinking: this is one of those moments when everything is perfect. You know you married the right guy, you know that you are a great parent with incredible kids, and you know you are going to make it in this world. And that was enhanced by the sun, the breeze, and such incredible farm-to-table food. So, thank you, Petite Pois, for putting so much passion in your food. Without it, it would have just been another ordinary day. ◆

The Family Picnic

THIS STORY IS SPONSORED BY

Southern Environmental Law Center

ON A SUNNY SPRING AFTERNOON, CALE JAFFE AND HIS WIFE, KATIE, HELP THEIR THREE
CHILDREN SPREAD A PICNIC BLANKET ON A GRASSY HILL ABOVE A FARM IN WESTERN
ALBEMARLE COUNTY. ON THE DAY'S MENU IS A LONGTIME FAMILY STANDBY.

"Whether we're hiking up along the Moormans River, climbing Spy Rock, or paddling Ivy Creek, we like to hit Bodo's on our way out of town," Cale says. The kids all have their go-to favorites. David is a purist: cream cheese on cinnamon raisin. Eliza always chooses turkey and Swiss on an everything bagel.

On their way to the hilltop, they hike through the woods, rock-hop along a creek, and admire passing goldfinches. They are barely ten minutes outside of Charlottesville, and the vista opens before them. When they arrive at the picnic spot, everyone is hungry, and the sandwiches disappear quickly.

"Charlottesville/Albemarle is such a special area," Cale says. "We have beautiful, rural countryside all around us. We have Shenandoah National Park and the George Washington National Forest right up the road. Many of the headwaters of the Rivanna, James, and Potomac Rivers come down right out of those mountains. Katie and I want our kids to be aware of all this."

Of all people, Cale knows that having healthy air, clean water, and intact, scenic landscapes doesn't happen by chance. As director of the Southern Environmental Law Center's Virginia office, Cale does more than just enjoy the open spaces: he works tirelessly to protect them.

Many in Charlottesville know SELC as the dedicated, hometown group that has opposed a western bypass that would encourage sprawling development and lead to loss of open space and farmland. But SELC's reach is much broader. For more than twenty-five years, SELC's team of top-notch attorneys has successfully used the power of the law to champion the natural resources of Virginia and five other southeast states.

SELC has two offices in Charlottesville, including its headquarters, and additional offices in Richmond; Washington, D.C.; Chapel Hill; Asheville; Charleston; Nashville; Atlanta; and Birmingham. This nonprofit works in all three branches of government to create, strengthen, and enforce the laws and policies put in place to protect our health and environment.

In Virginia, SELC is playing a central role in every major environmental challenge affecting the state. "It's hard to believe, but the Forest Service is considering allowing large-scale gas drilling and fracking for natural gas in the G.W. National

> *"I want my children to grow up with a strong sense of place, with an appreciation for what is authentic."*

Forest." Cale says. "We're weighing in to convince them to keep these public lands as wild and as beautiful as possible." SELC is also defending a 30-year-old ban on uranium mining in Virginia and working on multiple fronts to restore the Chesapeake Bay to health. The group aims to lead Virginia toward a cleaner energy future—including using its law and policy expertise to promote the speedy development of wind and solar power.

Back at the hilltop, it's time for the Jaffe family to shake off the blanket and start making their way back to the car. The kids clamber over a cattle gate.

"I want my children to grow up with a strong sense of place, with an appreciation for what is authentic," Cale says. These are values at the very heart of SELC's mission.

Today, for the Jaffes, it's an al fresco lunch on a hillside that captures what's quintessentially Charlottesville. At other times in the summer, it might mean hitting the City Market on a Saturday morning to score local produce, Caromont Farm goat cheese, or fresh doughnuts.

The Jaffes' oldest daughter, Caroline, is already thinking ahead to fall and the annual Vintage Virginia Apple Festival in Nelson County. The talk turns to hay rides, fresh cider, and the trunkful of apples the family usually totes home. "I wish," she tells her dad, "we could go there right now." ◆

MUST-HAVE PICNIC ITEMS
Bodo's Bagels

apples

cookies from Albemarle Baking Co.

FAVORITE OUTDOOR SPOTS
Sugar Hollow

Observatory Hill

Spy Rock

Beagle Gap in
Shenandoah National Park

SUMMER INGREDIENT

FIGS

Grilled Fig and Gorgonzola Dolce Salad

"insalata di fico alla griglia"

Michael Keaveny | tavola

INGREDIENTS

figs, cut in half
baby arugula
Gorgonzola Dolce
extra virgin olive oil
good balsamic vinegar
salt and pepper, to taste

DIRECTIONS

Lightly season 3 fig halves with salt and black pepper and grill flesh side down.

Toss handful of baby arugula in high-quality, fruity extra virgin olive oil, salt and black pepper. Place in center of plate.

Arrange 3 fig pieces (flesh side showing) to lean against each of three sides of the arugula. Place slice of Gorgonzola Dolce leaning on fourth side. Drizzle of aged balsamic vinegar around outside of plate. Simple elegance!

Stuffed Figs

Gayane Avagyan | Double H Farm

INGREDIENTS

24 fresh figs
1 c chopped walnuts
½ c raisins
2 T honey
1 t brandy or vanilla extract
¼–½ t ground cloves

DIRECTIONS

Using a small knife, make a small hole at the round end of each fig. Mix the ingredients together and insert one teaspoon of the stuffing into the fig. You can serve them fresh or bake at 350° F for 8-10 minutes.

A Local Feast

IT IS THE BEGINNING OF A BEAUTIFUL SUMMER EVENING WHEN WE MEET
SHEILA CAMP MOTLEY AND MATHEW ALLEN AT SHEILA'S FAMILY FARM FOR A MEAL SET
AMID THE ROLLING HILLS OF KESWICK, VIRGINIA. MAT, A CHEF, HAS PREPARED A MEAL FILLED WITH
LOCAL FAVORITES AND SHEILA, AN EVENT PLANNER, HAS SET A COTTAGE FARM TABLE WITH
LOCAL SUMMER FLOWERS FROM SOUTHERN BLOOMS AND VIBRANT CHINA FROM FESTIVE FARE.

We sit down to a meal as rich in local ingredients as it is in flavor, including arugula from Double H Farm, Bloomsbury cheese from Caromont Farm, short ribs from Best of What's Around, roasted chicken from Polyface, and wines from neighboring Keswick Vineyard.

Sheila and Mat's professional collaboration goes back many years, to when Sheila was a senior event planner at The Event Company in Charlottesville and Mat was a chef at a number of local favorites, including The X Lounge. Now married with a young son, they make their home in South Florida, where Mat is a sous chef for a caterer and Sheila has her own event company. They return to Virginia often to visit Sheila's family, and this summertime trip gave them perfect opportunity to collaborate again, with this lovely meal the result. ◆

MENU

*Double H Farm arugula with Caromont Farm
Bloomsbury cheese and herbed vinaigrette*

*beer-braised Best of What's Around short rib
with Wade's Mill stone-ground grits and
shaved Double H Farm carrot slaw*

*Polyface Farm roasted chicken with roasted
Double H Farm carrot and summer courgette*

Double H Farm cherry tart

◆ ◆ ◆

*2011 Norton – Keswick Vineyards
2011 Viognier – Keswick Vineyards*

RECIPES ON PAGE 146 + 147

Virginia Food Roots

Food can be as important to our memory of a place as its people or its landscape. Think of New Orleans, Italy, or France: our mental image of these places revolves around the cuisine served there. Craig Hartman hopes to create the same kind of strong identification between food and place in Central Virginia, too, and he hopes to do it with barbecue.

Craig spent decades as an executive chef in top-rated restaurants, including those at Clifton Inn and Keswick Hall, during which time he developed an interest in trying to capture the soul of Virginia cuisine.

While he was working at Clifton Inn, he began to conduct research to understand more about this area's distinctive dishes. He drove up and down the Route 231 corridor, from Shadwell to Sperryville, visiting hunt clubs in the area, which often carry detailed records of what was served in homes and estates there. The historical menus of these places had some distinctive features, but he quickly discerned that with items like pineapples and Belon oysters, they did not feature a great deal of Virginia-sourced food, and therefore were lacking in what could be considered authentic Virginia cuisine.

His initial attempts to mimic the food served at these places led him to what now identifies as "continental cuisine." By the time he was overseeing the kitchen at Keswick Hall, he realized that he'd missed a vital ingredient in this quest, and to find it, he needed to delve into the cuisine of the African American community.

"The food that comes from the earth and from the cultures of the people created this southern cuisine," Craig says. A centerpiece of this is cured and smoked meat, as both forms of preservation were vital to keeping meat on the table for those that worked the land.

At The Barbeque Exchange restaurant in Gordonsville, which Craig and his wife Donna opened in 2011, Craig focuses on getting the meat right. The restaurant's barbecues and smokers are fired only by wood—native Virginia green hickory, to be exact—rather than a hybrid of gas or electric and wood. The restaurant sources as much pork as possible from Virginia farms, including The Rock Barn, Timbercreek, and Autumn Olive, and Craig and his crew break down the sides of pork in-house, using as much of the animal as they can and making pulled pork, pork belly, bacon, country ham, sausage, and scrapple. They use a seasoning rub for the barbecue and a salt cure rub for the bacon, modeled on traditional methods. The restaurant's sides—including its cornbread, hushpuppies, slaws, and pickles—are also based on authentic Virginia recipes. Craig hopes this leads to an culinary experience that feels unique to Central Virginia—one that visitors can savor, and remember, long after they depart. ◆

RECIPE ON PAGE 147

Virginia's Bountiful Table

BY LENI SORENSEN, CULINARY HISTORIAN

THIS STORY IS SPONSORED BY
Craig + Donna Hartman

From the earliest days of the eighteenth century, the foods served in Virginia were lauded by residents and visitors alike. Oysters, cream, butter, many kinds of vegetables, wheat breads and corn breads, jellies and jams, and elaborate punches like the frothy wine-based syllabub continued to be popular for over two hundred years. Central Virginia and the Piedmont came to be seen as particularly rich in food resources. Orchards full of apples and peaches, Muscadine grapes, and fine beef and pork were hallmarks of the gentry plantation. From Mary Randolph and her dining table in Richmond of the 1810s to the Orange County kitchen in which Chef Edna Lewis learned her African American family's foodway traditions in the early twentieth century, words like *rich, beautiful, tasty,* and *bountiful* combine with more practical terms like *homegrown* and *homemade* to describe the food we cherish as *Virginian* today.

The most important thing to know about the roots of Virginia cuisine is that, be it the groaning board menus of the eighteenth century or the French-in-spired delicacy of the Monticello dinner table, it has always embodied a tradition of generous hospitality. As Katharine Harbury says in *Colonial Virginia's Cooking Dynasty*, "No hostess would want to risk the family's standing by being seen as lagging behind with respect to the latest fashion," be it in serving utensils, dining room furniture, or items on the menu (48). Indeed, even when guests were irritating, the Virginia hostess had to appear welcoming. Harbury details how in 1828, Alicia Middleton wrote to her son confiding about one of her guests, "He is really a bore he comes here just as if it were a tavern Friday afternoon without any invitation & stays until Monday it is too tiresome—Izard says Ma can't You tell him to go—" (50).

The dinners Mrs. Middleton served would have included the best foodstuffs in as much variety as possible but, as Harbury notes, "as the ultimate status symbol, the amount and variety of meats formed the dividing line between the gentry and the lower classes" (47). In the housekeep-

ing book of an anonymous gentry woman of the Randolph clan written in 1700, Harbury shows us the richness of her ideals of a proper meal presentation:

"The first Course

Potages—two sort of potages, vis a bisque of pigeon, and a potage de Sante, with a young fat hen

The Side Dishes—A quarter of mutton forced [this would have weighed about eight to ten pounds]; A large fat Pullet in a Ragoo; a breast of Veal forced [this meant chopped finely, pounded in a mortar, and pushed through a sieve for the smoothest of texture; the meat was then used as stuffing or formed into balls to be poached and served on a platter, often with a sauce]; Pigeons with sweet Basil in their bodies, together with a small farce [another name for stuffing or forced meat] and a large piece of Beef in the middle

The second Course

For the Roast; A great dish of roast-meat consisting of several fowls according to their season and two Sallets

The intermesses; A dish or Pain de Jambon [it would have been an unusual meal at which pork did not make an appearance]; Boil'd Cream; A ragoo of Sweet breads of veal and Capons-livers; A dish of asparagus with sauce of Jus lie , [Espagnole sauce made from veal or chicken bones without flour, thickened with arrowroot or cornflour, simmered briefly, seasoned and strained], or thick Gravy; and so there may be seven dishes for each Course" (48-9).

In ever-accelerating influence among the Virginia gentry during the eighteenth century, French cooking, or at least French names for particular dishes, became more common. Amid the alliance with France during the Revolutionary era, many a French general came to Virginia bringing their servants, especially their cooks. Moreover, during the Haitian War for Inde-

enslaved cooks. Virginia foodways historian Nancy Carter Crump summarizes this culinary encounter well in *Hearthside Cooking*: "Black cooks excelled in blending spices and other seasonings to create the exotic sauces of their culinary heritage. Essential flavorings in their cooking, many of which were already known to the English settlers, included ginger, saffron, thyme, sage, sweet basil, parsley, and especially shallot, as well as various hot peppers" (25). Africans introduced to the English colony watermelon, yams, rice, okra, and black-eyed peas—all foods that be-

---

"It is the image of gracious hospitality and abundance that has continued to characterize Virginia cooking from the earliest days to the present."

---

pendence—from 1791 to 1804—hundreds of exiled French planters from Haiti arrived in the Chesapeake with servants and cooks in tow to set up households. Gentry Virginians were entertained in those homes and many experienced French cooking for the first time. Thomas Jefferson's admiration for French cuisine was well developed before he went to France—witness his determination to take along one of his slaves to be trained in that art.

Along with the tremendous influence of French cookery in the homes of Virginia's gentry had come the African influence of

came important in the diets of all Virginians, rich and poor, black and white, enslaved and free. And to further create new layers of complexity, many of the enslaved African cooks of the seventeenth and early eighteenth centuries arrived after spending years in the kitchens of the Caribbean gentry, adding native Carib, Arawak Indian, Spanish, and Dutch flavors to the Virginia culinary palette.

But it is the image of gracious hospitality and abundance that has continued to characterize Virginia cooking from the earliest days to the present. As detailed by Crump, at George Washington's Mount Vernon on a June afternoon in 1797, one guest noted, "The diner was very good—a small roasted pig, boiled leg of lamb, beef, peas, lettuce, cucumbers, artichokes, etc., puddings, tarts, etc. We were desired to call for what drink we chose" (45). Born in the early twentieth century, Chef Edna Lewis was taught by expert cooks, gardeners, and farmers, often ex-slaves—people deeply steeped in the finest Virginia country culinary tradition. In *The Taste of Country Cooking*, she told of a menu for a Sunday Revival dinner that resembled in variety and quantity the gentry dinners of a hundred years before: at a time of year when the garden and field were at their most prolific, the menu was baked Virginia ham, Southern fried chicken, braised leg of mutton, sweet potato casserole, corn pudding, green beans with pork, platters of sliced tomatoes with dressing, spiced Seckel pears, cucumber pickles, yeast rolls, biscuits, sweet potato pie, summer apple pie, Tyler pie (much like a Shoo Fly pie), caramel layer cake, lemonade, and iced tea (116).

A more secular dining experience was to be had at any respectable political rally or Election Day well into the twentieth century. Whole-hog barbecue, often with a dozen or more hogs, would be prepared in long trenches by skilled black pitmasters. Dolley Madison, at her Montpelier estate, understood the delight with which her guests greeted the fabulous smells of several hogs roasting over a fire. Her summer feasts often included over a hundred people. Such spectacular barbecue presentations were the culinary centerpiece of weddings and the Fourth of July.

When the bell was rung to call people to the table, whether a small family or a party of several hundred, cured ham and roasted or barbecued pork always had a central place at the table. These beautiful dishes, surrounded by the richness of other food harvested and prepared in the Virginia countryside then expertly accented with the savors of spices from afar, showed that Virginians have always know how to eat well. ◆

 RECIPES ON PAGE 147

BOOKS REFERENCED IN THIS ESSAY

"Colonial Virginia's Cooking Dynasty," by Katharine E. Harbury. Columbia: The University of South Carolina Press, 2004.

"Hearthside Cooking: Early American Southern Cuisine Updated for Today's Hearth and Cookstove," by Nancy Carter Crump. 2nd ed. Chapel Hill: The University of North Carolina Press, 2008.

"The Taste of Country Cooking," by Edna Lewis. New York: Random House LLC, 2006.

CVILLE SAMPLER

Anita Gupta | Owner, Maliha Creations

For a dear friend's fortieth birthday, we struggled to figure out a unique way to celebrate. In the past, we had marked such occasions with parties, brunches, wine tastings, and dinners out, but we knew we needed to do something different since it was a special birthday. Together, the four of us are always game for trying out new restaurants and unique flavors, but the thought of "just a dinner out" seemed redundant and not entirely special. Uday and I finally settled on the idea of a progressive dinner on our wonderful Downtown Mall.

Uday headed to the three restaurants that we chose prior to dinner and decorated our tables with balloons and streamers. The best part was that each restaurant was totally on board with our idea and did not have a problem with us eating only one course there. The servers were awesome in helping our celebrations move smoothly, especially since our guests did not know what the evening was going to entail. Our evening began at Bang!, where we enjoyed delicious summer martinis with a variety of appetizers. From our asparagus spring rolls to the kale raviolis, everything was fresh and delicious. The laughter and banter came easily as we shared little bites of the Asian-inspired tapas.

Now that we were not overly ravenous, we were able to finish our cocktails and began a leisurely stroll over to the Commonwealth Restaurant & SkyBar. Uday had decked out one of the circular booths with more balloons and streamers. The large windows facing the booths were open and we enjoyed the cool breeze from outside. The ladies started with a crisp sauvignon blanc and the gentlemen tried some of the signature cocktails. While the appetizers looked lovely, we moved onto to the dinner portion of our meal. With around eight entrees to choose from, we definitely had some choices to make. As always, we decided to each choose a different entrée so we could each have a little taste of something different. We chose the sea bass, the pork chop, the skirt steak and the jambalaya. Each dish was completely composed and so unique from each other. We enjoyed our meals completely and lingered over our wine. Since we had some space between courses, we were not overly stuffed as we sometimes felt and knew we would have some room for dessert.

By now, night was falling and the evening was quite pleasant and beautiful. We made our way over to C&O Restaurant and headed to the back patio, where our final table of the evening was waiting for us. We settled on a beautifully crimson rosé sparkling wine. It was slightly sweet, but not overly so and went perfectly with the chocolate brioche bread pudding and the Coupe Maison, the house-churned ice cream with toasted almonds and chocolate sauce. We lingered over our bubbly and enjoyed each other's company as we toasted another year older. We were pleasantly full and needed the walk up the hill to our car parked near Bang!

In the span of four hours, we were able to eat at some of our favorite restaurant spots in Charlottesville. While we would have fully enjoyed an entire evening at each of these restaurants on their own merit, it was nice to extend the evening, have an element of surprise for our guests, and get a taste of all of the wonderfulness our town has to offer. I can say without a doubt, we will be doing this again with other restaurants. ◆

Cville Classics

A glimpse of three iconic Charlottesville eateries

TIMBERLAKE'S

It doesn't get much more local than Timberlake's Drug Store & Soda Fountain, which opened in downtown Charlottesville in 1890. Originally located across the street, Timberlake's moved to its current location on East Main Street in 1917. Among its longest-serving employees are Millie Carter, an employee of the store since 1958, and Constance Mays, who has been working there since 1969.

In the back of the store, the soda fountain serves up lunch daily, featuring homemade items like baked turkey breast, barbecue, chili, and pimento cheese. But the star of the show may well be the thick, delicious milkshakes, which come in three standard flavors—chocolate, vanilla, and strawberry—as well as seasonal flavors, like peppermint and peach. ◆

LOCAL FAVORITES

house-roasted turkey

pimento cheese

milkshakes

MEL'S CAFE

Over on West Main Street, tucked among the blocks of restaurants and shops, is a little diner that has been gracing this neighborhood for more than twenty years: Mel's Cafe. Named after owner Mel Walker, who mans the grill, Mel's Cafe seeks to offer its patrons "down-to-earth, home-cooked food." With a menu full of comfort food favorites, it meets this goal, and then some.

"We try to treat everyone nice and offer good service," Mel says matter-of-factly. "We meet a lot of people from all of the world; people come from everywhere and we just talk to to them and share stories. That's a big part of it."

One thing Mel doesn't share is how to make the restaurant's sweet potato pie—it's his grandma's secret recipe! ◆

LOCAL FAVORITES

burgers
fried chicken
sweet potato pie

SPUDNUTS

Just over the Belmont bridge on the edge of downtown is a Charlottesville staple: The Spudnut Shop, which has been serving up doughnuts in this location since 1969. Lori and Mike Fitzgerald own the shop, which was originally opened as a franchise by Lori's parents. You can find the Fitzgeralds there every day; in fact, Mike arrives at 2 a.m. to start the day's batches.

Made with potato flour, the doughnuts fly off the shelves and into the hands of a constant stream of local patrons, most of whom will take them to work or home to enjoy. There's usually a table or two filled with other frequent customers, who linger over cups of coffee long after their breakfast treats have been devoured. If you're lucky, you can get there right as a fresh batch is carried out from the kitchen, and savor the heavenly taste of a hot Spudnut doughnut. There is truly nothing else like it. ◆

LOCAL FAVORITES
blueberry
chocolate glazed
plain glazed

Local Food in Local Hands

THIS STORY IS SPONSORED BY

Feast!

This is the story of two tomatoes. The first is sitting in a large, clean plastic tub with several dozen others, all mouthwateringly red and ripe. On a long table next to the tomatoes are other bins of beautiful, fresh produce, washed and piled in open-topped boxes for easy perusal—cucumbers, green beans, peppers, and summer squash, among others. Around it, a crowd of people is gathering on this August afternoon, each carrying a bag—be it plastic, paper, or cloth—that they intend to fill with fresh, organic vegetables. The feeling of anticipation among the men, women, and children in the group is palpable.

This tomato is part of the weekly market held by the Urban Agriculture Collective of Charlottesville (UACC) on Friday afternoons in the courtyard of Crescent Hall, near downtown Charlottesville. It started as a seedling planted in one of the gardens by Todd Niemeier—the director of UACC's gardens, often called "Farmer Todd"—or by one of the dozens of volunteers over the growing season that come to assist in this effort. These individuals helped to weed and mulch around the tomato plant to ensure that it thrived. When its fruit was finally ripe, one of these volunteers helped to harvest it, and added it to offerings at this week's market.

UACC is a nonprofit organization set up in 2012 to manage a collection of urban gardens in the Friendship Court, 6th Street, and West Street neighborhoods, which combined produce an average of 10,000 pounds of organic fruits and vegetables each year on a half-acre of land. Since the urban gardens were established in 2007, dozens of volunteers from the neighborhoods surrounding these gardens and from all over Charlottesville have contributed nearly 3,000 hours of service in the form of planting, weeding, harvesting, and distribution. Those who volunteer earn a wooden token for each half-hour of time and can exchange the token for vegetables at the weekly market, held at Crescent Hall, or share their tokens with those in the community who would benefit from the produce, but have been unable to volunteer time.

Within minutes of the market opening, the tomato is chosen from the pile by an elderly woman who lives right here at Crescent Hall. This market allows her access to fresh, organic produce—access she might otherwise not have. There are dozens of volunteers helping to bring this dream of fresh food for all to life, and among them is Kate Collier, co-owner with her husband Eric Gertner of Feast!, a specialty food shop and café located in the Main Street Market building on West Main Street in Charlottesville. Kate became involved with UACC a couple of years ago, after accompanying her son Oscar on a kindergarten field trip to the gardens. She was especially impressed by Farmer Todd, who explained to the students the benefits of harvesting rainwater, and how certain plants can help naturally manage garden pests.

"I love volunteering with UACC because Oscar and I can do it together and we always meet lots of new children. We can go and pull up garlic for two hours, load six bins on Farmer Todd's trailer and leave feeling productive and happy every time," says Kate, who now serves on an eight-member volunteer board that helps to oversee the nonprofit. "UACC is special because it brings all sorts of folks together to build community gardens in urban Charlottesville. The organic food from those gardens is then made available to garden volunteers and seniors at Crescent Hall. It is from seed to table within a few urban blocks!"

Kate and Eric launched Feast in early 2002, driven by a desire to put Virginia-made products into the hands of more Virginia residents, thereby supporting local vendors and food producers in as direct a way as possible. Both grew up in families with a strong connection to food. Eric spent formative years in Eau Claire, Wisconsin, gardening and putting up the harvest at home and on the farms of his aunts and uncles, and bagging groceries and stocking shelves at the local independent grocer, Kerm's Super Foods. These experiences taught him the value of cooperation and community, and gave root to his love of food. Kate was raised in Fauquier County, Virginia, with two parents in the food business: her father ran a restaurant with a seasonally inspired menu, while her mother ran a business making shortbread and chocolate out of a converted machine shed on the family's property. When Kate was eleven, she started going to food shows with her mother, helping represent her mother's product. Through this she met scores of other Virginia food producers and their families.

"A lot of artisan foods are produced by families," Kate says, noting that what attracted her and Eric to this industry was an understanding that the best thing they could do to support businesses and families making food was to buy, market, and promote their products.

"We thought we could offer customers a value-added experience by telling them the story of the people who produced the food," she says of Feast!, which has expanded to three times its original size since opening its doors more than a decade ago. As the store became more established and the number of local farmers they knew grew, Kate and Eric kept hearing a common theme: these farmers were spending a lot of time driving to farmer's markets and small retailers like Feast!—time they needed to be spending producing and cultivating the food that sustained their livelihood.

At the same time, Feast! was fielding calls from commercial clients who were in-

> *"If we want food producers and farmers in our area to get their food into the mouths of our community, we need to create fair access to the markets that exist here."*

terested in utilizing more locally produced food, but didn't know where to start. Kate and Eric saw a disconnect between farmers, who needed larger accounts, and businesses, which needed a reliable supply of locally sourced food. The answer they came up with to solve this disconnect was the Local Food Hub. Founded in 2009, this nonprofit serves as a distribution service for local farmers, connecting large accounts like local hospitals and schools with locally grown food.

"If we want food producers and farmers in our area to get their food into the mouths of our community, we need to create fair access to the markets that exist here," Eric says. "While farmers' markets and CSAs do a wonderful job of this, access to traditional channels that sell to stores, restaurants and institutions have largely disappeared, replaced by a system of trade that emphasizes price and seasonally-blind supply. Both Feast! and the Hub are focused on reversing this trend by generating consistent and exuberant demand for foods made by hand and grown by our neighbors."

And this brings us to our second tomato, delivered to Local Food Hub on a Monday morning in August by a local farmer. It was grown at a small farm south of Charlottesville, by a farmer who is working land that has been in her family for generations. This farmer has been through a lengthy paperwork process and a farm visit by Local Food Hub staff, so the ins and outs of her farm operation are well known. The tomato and the others the farmer harvested early that morning are examined by Local Food Hub staff. If any are not quite suitable for distribution, they are set aside and donated to the Blue Ridge Food Bank. Those ready for distribution are packaged and labeled with the farm's name and the date they were delivered to Local Food Hub. Though they may be temporarily stored there at the distribution center, most will quickly find their way to commercial clients on Local Food Hub's distribution truck, which makes deliveries on weekdays.

This tomato and many others from local farms are loaded into the Local Food Hub's truck and taken over to the University of Virginia Health System. There it may become part of a salad or a sandwich for one of the hospital's staff or patients, creating an important and mutually beneficial connection, in which one small tomato provides meaningful sustenance to many. ◆

The Sweet Spot

THIS STORY IS SPONSORED BY
Gearharts Fine Chocolates

THIS WEEKDAY AFTERNOON IN CHARLOTTESVILLE HAS THE USUAL HALLMARKS OF LATE JUNE:
BLAZING HEAT, AMPLE HUMIDITY, AND THE KINETIC ENERGY OF SUMMER IN A COLLEGE TOWN.
IN A SHOP IN THE MAIN STREET MARKET BUILDING ON WEST MAIN, SNEAKERS COME POUNDING DOWN
A WIDE STAIRCASE—PAIR AFTER PAIR, BELONGING TO CHILD AFTER CHILD DRESSED IN COLORFUL
T-SHIRTS, ALL JABBERING EXCITEDLY, FINISHING A TOUR OF GEARHARTS FINE CHOCOLATES.

They tromp down the steps from the production kitchen above in a seemingly endless stream, one by one taking their enthusiastic chatter out the glass door at the bottom of the steps, into the parking lot outside, and onto their next destination. When the last few depart, the shop is left to a handful of tourists. One gentleman stops to try a sample from a tray sitting on a cabinet next to the stairs, then gestures to his companions to do the same.

The chocolaterie is a small, simple space, with a few glass-front cabinets lining the walls displaying the shop's creations. The cabinet across the back holds a trove of chocolates with names like Earl Grey, Criolla, Maya, Taj, Brown Butter Caramel, and Mint Julep. They are uniform in presentation and lovely to behold. Gearharts will produce about 750,000 chocolates this year that will be purchased by locals, tourists, visitors, and customers who order them through the shop's website. Business is good.

But the story of this shop's success starts not in the production kitchen upstairs, but in another kitchen down the street, on the Downtown Mall. That is where Tim Gearhart met Bill Hamilton nearly 18 years ago, after answering an ad in the paper for a pastry chef position at a new restaurant. That restaurant would end up being Hamiltons' at First and Main. It would become an icon of Charlottesville's fine dining scene, and Tim Gearhart would become its first pastry chef.

Bill Hamilton and his wife Kate cooked up the idea for Hamiltons' in the mid 1990s, having worked at the now-shuttered Rococo's, where Bill was the chef and Kate was a front-of-house manager. They had a concept for a restaurant that would make everything in-house—long before the farm-to-table trend that is so prevalent in today's restaurant scene—and to accomplish this, one position they had to fill was that of pastry chef.

While Bill and Kate were working on bringing their idea of Hamiltons' to fruition, Tim was wrapping up an externship at Keswick Hall following culinary school. After five years in the Marine Corps, where he served as a cook, he had been among the second group to graduate from the Culinary Institute of America's nascent pastry arts program. As his time at Keswick came to a close, he answered Bill and Kate's ad for a pastry chef position at Hamiltons'. Bill knew immediately that he'd found the right person.

"It was a good fit," Bill says. "He had the culinary school experience. He was ready to take on some responsibility."

Hamiltons' opened on February 14, 1996. One of four fine dining restaurants on the Downtown Mall at that time, it quickly developed a devoted following. Tim manned the pastry chef role for a year and a half, developing the recipe for the house bread and the concept for the "Chocolate, Many Ways" dessert that Hamiltons' serves to this day. After helping to establish the restaurant, he felt the pull of new opportunities, and headed west to work in Wyoming, then over to a kitchen in Britain, the back to the States for a position in Boston. Five years passed.

With his parents still in central Virginia, Tim visited regularly and would often stop by Hamiltons' to see Bill. As the years passed, their conversations turned to developing a venture together. They thought

harts, which they launched in September. In each case, they partnered with individuals who worked for them at Hamiltons'.

"What we were able to do was bring some experience, some banking relationships and customer relationships," Bill says of these ventures. He notes that Hamiltons' clientele was uniquely helpful in getting

"The more important thing is finding people who are willing to try—and fail. It's a balance of humility and bravery. The bravery to actually do something, but the humility to know that you can't do everything, to know your weaknesses."

Charlottesville's strong appreciation of artisan food made it an ideal market for a boutique chocolate shop, which were at that time uncommon in the United States.

After amassing experience in several kitchens, Tim was ready to start something of his own. Bill, having successfully established Hamiltons' as a permanent fixture of the city's food scene, found himself at a crossroads; he and Kate needed to decide if they were going to continue to spend their careers in the trenches of the restaurant, or widen their business experience.

In 2001, Bill and Kate chose a path that led them to start not one but two new businesses: Sticks Kebob Shop, which opened on Preston Avenue in March, and Gear-

press for Gearharts and developing its initial customer base. The restaurant was the shop's first wholesale client, with chocolate from the shop appearing on the restaurant's dessert menu.

In the nearly two decades since Hamiltons' opened its doors, a lot of people have worked on the restaurant's front- and back-of-house operations. And while he has met scores of fascinating people this way, Bill acknowledges that only a few of these were right for a business partnership.

"The more important thing is finding people who are willing to try—and fail. It's a balance of humility and bravery. The bravery to actually do something, but the humility to know that you can't do everything, to

know your weaknesses," he says. He found that kind of person in Tim Gearhart.

Tim echoes this sentiment. His father, a business consultant, frequently told him that no matter which type of career you have, the key is to find the people who are the the best at what they do and surround yourself with them.

"Bill and Kate were a vision of what it can be: how to treat people and how to treat employees," Tim adds.

Because of the care Bill and Tim put into their partnership, in the twelve years since Gearharts opened, the biggest hurdles it has had to overcome have involved keeping up with demand. Tim notes that they can produce up to 9,000 chocolates in a given day at certain times of the year.

With a solid, established customer base, Tim and Bill are now able to focus attention on dreaming up new products, like Mas Guapo, an organic blend of spices and herbs that is gaining a cult following for its versatility in the kitchen. These projects offer them opportunities to exercise their creative muscle and try out new ideas.

Customers flow into Gearharts Fine Chocolates in a steady stream all afternoon. Each time, a bell rings in the production kitchen, where the stacks of signature dark-brown boxes speak to the success of not just one business, but two, and offer proof that at the intersection of hard work, skill, and vision, a sweet spot truly can exist. ◆

RECIPE ON PAGE 148

HEARTTHROB

Hunter Smith | President + Head Brewer, Champion Brewing Company

One experience that really made me beam was one of the first times I went to Glass Haus Kitchen. I tweeted Chef Boden to let him know I was in, and much to my surprise, out to the otherwise quiet bar came a special ramen dish that wasn't on the menu. A complete interpretation of a guinea hen was presented as a ramen bowl. It was unbelievable: poached egg and guinea hen sausage in a rich, simmering broth with fat, sticky noodles, replete with heart on a skewer. The heart was the first I'd ever had, and it blew my mind. I immediately remarked that it was the best piece of meat I've ever eaten, and I think that's still true. I was immediately pulled out of my comfort zone and had never been so glad I was.

Thanks to Ian's hospitable gesture, I am far more inclined to try new food items, particularly offal and other meats that are outside of the typical cuts that are served. The dark and intimate atmosphere of the late-night experience at Glass Haus feels juxtaposed with the diversity and intensity of its late-night menu. It still feels like a well-kept secret that some of the best food in town is hiding down the street, but it won't be for long. It may not be by the time I finish writing this. ◆

AMONG FRIENDS

Lynelle Lawrence | Director of Joy, Mudhouse Coffee Roasters

I have so many great food moments in Charlottesville; this town has a sophisticated and beautiful pallet. One of these is eating at a farm table inside The Bridge Progressive Arts Initiative for a gathering of about fifteen friends. We all shared a wonderful meal, which included a goat cooked on a pit in the parking lot in Belmont, courtesy of Rick Eastman. It was delicious. Delicious. While The Clash played softly in the background, we savored jugs of wine, wonderful side dishes, and finger nibbling-good goat. ◆

Farm Fresh & Frosted

THIS STORY IS SPONSORED BY
Sweethaus

Little boots tromp down a worn path on a summer morning, headed for the hen house. Their owners have come to collect eggs from a group of hens who live at this farm outside of Charlottesville. Inside the coop resides a flock of Red Stars, known for their tame and friendly dispositions. Little hands offer grain to inquisitive beaks. For some of these children, this is the first time they have interacted with chickens, but any trepidation is soon replaced by delight. After each has a chance to feed the hens, little fingers reach into nesting boxes to gather eggs.

"It's still warm!" a small voice exclaims.

◆ ◆ ◆

Little shoes gather in a half-circle around a low, long table. On the table sits a lavender KitchenAid mixer, a collection of mixing bowls, a couple dozen brown eggs lined up in an open egg crate, an old-fashioned hand-crank sifter, and a jar of organic milk. The same group of children that visited the farm this morning are here, in the party room at Sweethaus on West Main Street, to make a favorite treat: cupcakes. Behind the counter, Sweethaus owner Tara Koenig starts with cracking eggs, a guaranteed crowd-pleaser. One by one, little hands reach toward the beguiling eggs, select one and—crack!

While each child gets his or her turn with an egg, Tara reminds them of their trip to the farm that morning, helping the children draw a connection between the chickens they fed and eggs they collected, and the eggs they are adding to the batter. She points out the bright yellow-orange color of the yolk, a sure sign of a happy hen.

◆ ◆ ◆

Little shoes rock forward to tip-toes and little eyes peer into the hand-crank sifter as Tara fills it with cake flour, then passes it around the table. Small fingers grasp the sifter and turn the crank, sometimes with a little help from Tara. 'Round and 'round goes the crank, the flour falling gently down, down, down into the bowl beneath.

"It's snowing!" a small voice calls out.

The jar of milk needs something special to add the flavor. "Who knows what this is?" Tara asks, passing around a small glass bowl of dark brown liquid. A long pause follows.

"Vanilla...extract!" a small voice shouts.

While the mixer does its job, the baking pan is fitted with cupcake paper liners, one by one. Tara pours the batter into the cups, then pops the pan in the oven right there in the

party room. Little shoes rest on the rungs of stools set around the party table in the middle of the room, waiting for the cupcakes to finish and cool. During this pause, Tara loads up a half-dozen plastic sleeves with chocolate and vanilla icing, and gives each child a little cup with sprinkles and a sugar chicken figurine. When the cupcakes are ready, each pair of little hands gets one of their very own. Tara shows how to squeeze the frosting onto the top of the cupcake, and each child chooses the flavor they want.

"Look! I made a circle!" a little voice exclaims.

"It's a nest!" says another.

And now, the grand finale. Little hands lift frosting-laden cupcakes to little mouths, followed by a not-so-little chomp!

◆ ◆ ◆

This morning's festivities are part of Farm Fresh & Frosted, a new Sweethaus program aimed at promoting pasture-to-plate connections in an innovative way. Tara points out that the flagship farm-fresh items that excite adults—like tomatoes, green beans, or grass-fed beef—don't carry the same appeal for children. But something they can understand is the feeling of a warm egg in their hand, and then seeing the bright hue of a farm-fresh egg when it's cracked into a mixing bowl for cupcake batter.

"It's important for kids to learn that eggs and milk aren't born on grocery store shelves," Tara says. "Allowing them to create a tangible, edible, visually appealing cupcake out of ingredients they've hand-selected brings a heady concept down to their level."

This program, which was launched over the spring and summer of 2013, will offer groups of children and adults the opportunity to travel to local farms, interact with the animals there, and then create something using local ingredients—Sweethaus sources its eggs from Timbercreek Farm, for example—to create baked goods. And while this program is perfect for children, adults are very receptive to the concept, and have been eager to book Farm Fresh & Frosted trips for their own birthdays and even corporate team-building exercises.

"For adult groups, we can incorporate other farm ingredients, like chocolate-and-bacon cupcakes, which are a favorite for anyone who has tasted the salty-and-sweet combo," Tara says.

With its spacious event and playrooms and relaxed, vintage atmosphere, Sweethaus is known in the community as a terrific venue for parties. With Farm Fresh & Frosted, Tara hopes to take that success and provide participants with the experience of a farm, the connection to ingredients, and the excitement of an adventure—all in the three-hour timespan of a standard party. She notes that with its wealth of local farms right outside of town, Charlottesville is uniquely suited to making a program like Farm Fresh & Frosted a success.

One by one, little fingers are licked clean. Little hands are washed, little rain boots are donned and little feet tromp out to the parking lot and to awaiting cars, with a few puddle jumps along the way. Little tummies are full. Little mouths smile. Back in the party room at Sweethaus, a few sprinkles grace the table, a little reminder of a big day. ◆

"It's important for kids to learn that eggs and milk aren't born on grocery store shelves."

SWEET HEAT

Erica Hellen | Co-owner, Free Union Grass Farm

Joel and I don't normally go to town on Friday nights, because we're busy prepping for the Saturday farmers' market. But on one recent Friday, we were exhausted, desperate for something out of the ordinary, and had to buy dry ice. So we decided to make a quick trip into Charlottesville and try out Monsoon Siam.

This particular Friday was HOT, just the way we like it. We sat outside on Monsoon's eclectic little patio, enjoying the hustle and bustle of Market Street and the Downtown Mall on a weekend. We took our time perusing the extensive menu since we don't eat Thai food that often. Joel, in his typical fashion, asked the waiter for his opinion of the best thing on the menu. Given his recommendation, Joel ordered the kao pad ka pow and I asked for the yellow curry. The fun thing about Monsoon is that they can adjust the heat on any of the entrées upon request, so if you're not feeling as brave you can order it with one "chili pepper," and if you want to set your taste buds on fire, you can crank it up to four or five. We both nervously added a couple metaphorical peppers to our entrées and set about deciding on drinks.

On a hot summer night like this one, I wanted something with a lot of citrus to compliment the food, but with enough edge to stand on its own. I ordered a gin gimlet, thinking the lime would be a good accompaniment. The cool gin with the sweet-sour of the lime was the perfect match; it's rare I pick something that pairs so well with what I'm eating.

My curry was incredible. I'm a sucker for curry, but it doesn't always have that slight sweetness I like, and this one did. It's a simple dish, but it had plenty of texture, the right amount of heat, and gave me that warm feeling throughout. It's actually easier for me to enjoy the heat if I just keep eating it, so this wasn't a slow food experience. Joel's dish was also a success—the spicy basil sauce gave it a distinct Thai personality. The rice was perfectly cooked and the right amount of food for a hungry farmer. Joel has the adorable habit of hiccuping when he eats really hot food, and he did not disappoint. We finished our meals with the pleasant mouth buzz that spice brings, our lips visibly reddened but still smiling. We have been and will continue to go back— a summer food favorite! ◆

Old World Meets New

This is a coppa roll. The coppa, a cut from the pork shoulder, has long been an Italian favorite when cured, but it is typically overlooked in standard American butchery. Ben Thompson, founder and owner of The Rock Barn in Arrington, Virginia, is hoping to change that, and the coppa roll—in which the coppa cut is rolled up in its own layer of fat—is an example of how he hopes to do it.

"The coppa is quite possibly one of the best pieces of pure solid muscle meat you can eat; it has incredible marbling," he says, noting that in the USDA method of butchery, you would cut right through the coppa. To get at the coppa and other cuts like it, Ben uses a different approach.

"USDA cut theory is basically built on a chop-shop style of doing things," he explains. "Old-world butchery comes from craftsmen that have generations of training and tradition and culture that have informed them how to do their job. USDA cut is more factory-based, bringing in the cheapest labor possible, giving them a machine and teaching them to do it right away—eliminating the need for that generational knowledge or culture or history or respect."

Instead, Ben looks back to an older, European style of butchery, which emphasizes nose-to-tail principles. "On the USDA side, the principals they look for are cheaper and cheaper ways to do it because you just need to increase volume in order to keep up," he says. "On the European side, you have a finite amount of animals and space; you don't have the option of just ramping up volume, so you look at how to get more money out of each cut."

Ben came to the art of butchery from the world of culinary arts. A former ship's cook in the Navy and a graduate of the Culinary Institute of America, he worked in two of Thomas Keller's restaurants—per se in Manhattan and The French Laundry in California's Napa Valley—before moving with his wife Reagan to Arrington, in Nelson County, south of Charlottesville, in 2009 and launching The Rock Barn. This background as a chef informs Ben's thinking when it comes to the art of butchery.

"One thing that's exciting to us as butchers is some of the larger-format items that make for cool family-style presentations that maybe people haven't seen before," he says. "To me as a chef, those things are very exciting, because there's only so many ways you can cook a pork chop; there are only so many ways you can do barbecue."

It is this search that led him to the coppa roll, a confluence of lean muscle meat and fat that is truly greater than the sum of its parts, with the fat rendering into the meat as it cooks, permeating it with flavor and tenderizing it in the process. After trying it out a few times himself, Ben is now offering this cut to customers interested in trying something out of the ordinary. It is this marriage of old-world butchery tech-

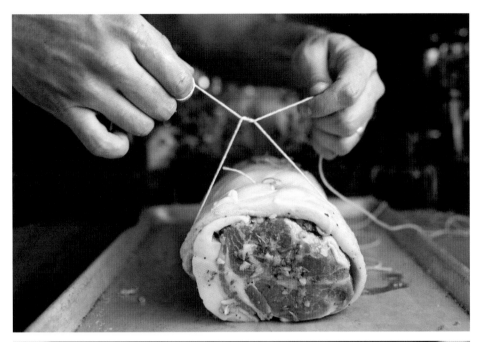

niques with innovative new products that has gained The Rock Barn an enthusiastic following in Charlottesville's food community. Chefs swear by Ben's products, and customers who stop at The Rock Barn's stall on Saturdays at the City Market are bound to walk away with newfound knowledge and meat cuts new and old, as well as ideas for preparing them.

To cook the coppa roll, Ben suggests a dry rub tailored to the season. For spring or summer, think tender green garlic cloves, mashed in a mortar and pestle with fresh, chopped marjoram, salt, white pepper, and fresh ginger. This is spread on the muscle a full twenty-four hours ahead of smoking, and then the fat is wrapped around it and the roll is tied with butcher's string. This kind of cut is best cooked slowly over low heat—about 225 degrees Farenheit—and then finished over higher heat for the last ten minutes to create a crisper outer layer.

To complement the coppa roll for a spring or summer meal, he recommends a quick pickling of garlic scapes the day before, then cutting the pickled scapes on the bias into small pieces. While the grill is fired up to cook the coppa roll, it can also grill some yellow freestone peaches, cut in half and grilled cut-side down for a few minutes. These can be set aside with the pickling juice for the garlic scapes poured over top and allowed to rest for about a half-hour.

For the presentation, Ben recommends a bed of arugula dressed with olive oil and a hard crystal sea salt. The chopped, pickled garlic scapes are sprinkled over this bed and the peaches are placed around the perimeter. The coppa roll sits in the middle.

With a side of green beans almondine, dinner is served.

On a summer Sunday afternoon, we cook the coppa roll and serve it just as Ben advises, smoking it for eight hours in a Big Green Egg over low heat, its juices dripping into the pan below. Its smell is a heavenly meeting of a roast and barbecue—sweet, smoky, rich, and warm. Sitting on the grill, it looks and smells every bit the main attraction of a celebratory meal.

We sit outside on a warm evening following a day of thunderstorms, enjoying a break in the storm clouds and the long, luscious light of evening. The meat is dense, yet the outer layer of fat has left it tender. The fat that remains easily falls away as we cut the coppa roll slices on our plates. With its rich flavor, it is the ideal centerpiece to a Sunday meal. Sweet peaches, slightly bitter arugula and tangy pickled garlic scapes complement the meat as ideally as Ben had envisioned. Plates are filled, emptied and filled again, with every bit devoured. We all agree that this first coppa roll is a resounding success. It will not be our last. ◆

SEASONAL VARIATIONS

Late Summer
Stuff the coppa roll with pine nuts and currants.
Serve with ratatouille and orzo.

Fall
Stuff the coppa roll with pecan and cranberry chutney. Serve with roasted Brussels sprouts and a garnet yam puree.

Winter
Marinate the coppa roll with rosemary and roasted garlic. Serve with savory chestnut bread pudding, braising greens and orange supremes.

PICK YOUR OWN

· CENTRAL VIRGINIA ·

N

29/15

CULPEPPER

HARRISONBURG

ELKTON

33

33

(23)

(22)

29

ORANGE

522

(21)
(20)
(19)

UNIONVILLE

(1)

340

(18)
(17)

20

81

15

GORDONSVILLE

522

(6) (7) (8)
(5)

WAYNESBORO   CROZET

29

20

33

STAUNTON

(2)

(3)
(4)

340

CHARLOTTESVILLE

(16)

29

(9)

(15)

15

250

(10)

COVESVILLE

PALMYRA

64

(11)

(13)
(12)

LOVINGSTON

(24)

(14)

FARM LISTING

1. MIDDLE RIVER FARMS

1744 Weyers Cave Road
Grottoes, VA 24441

[strawberries]

2. TROYER NURSERY

66 Conner Road
Waynesboro, VA 22980

[strawberries]

3. CRITZER FAMILY FARM

9388 Critzer Shop Road
Route 151
Afton, VA 22920

[strawberries]

4. a.m. FOG

9264 Critzer's Shop Road
Afton, VA 22920

[veggies, raspberries, & pumpkins]

5. CHILES PEACH ORCHARD

1351 Greenwood Road
Crozet, VA 22932

[apples, peaches, pumpkins, & strawberries]

6. WAYLAND ORCHARD

6474 Apple Green Lane
Crozet, VA 22932

[apples]

7. HENLEY'S ORCHARD

2192 Holly Hill Farm
Crozet, VA 22932

[nectarines, peaches, & apples]

8. THE BERRY PATCH

3035 Pevine Hollow
Free Union, VA 22932

[blueberries, raspberries, & blackberries]

9. SPRING VALLEY ORCHARD

3526 Spring Valley Road
Afton, VA 22920

[cherries]

10. HILL TOP BERRY FARM & WINERY

2800 Berry Hill Road
Nellysford, VA 22958

[blueberries & blackberries]

11. DICKIE BROS. ORCHARD

2552 Dickie Road
Roseland, VA 22967

[apples, nectarines, peaches, & pumpkins]

12. SEAMANS' ORCHARD

415 Dark Hollow Road
Roseland, VA 22967

[strawberries, cherries, blueberries, & apples]

13. MOUNTAIN COVE ORCHARD

108 Banton Orchard Lane
Lovingston, VA 22949

[apples]

14. GRUNT N GOBBLE FARM

1366 Hundley Branch Road
Scottsville, VA 24590

[blueberries]

15. BELLAIR FARM CSA

5375 Bellair Farm
Charlottesville, VA 22902

[seasonal produce]

16. CARTER MOUNTAIN ORCHARD

1435 Carters Mountain Trail
Charlottesville, VA 22901

[apples, nectarines, & peaches]

17. GRELEN NURSERY

15111 Yager Road
Somerset, VA 22972

[blackberries, blueberries, raspberries (red), raspberries (yellow), & raspberries (black)]

18. GOLD HILL BLUEBERRY FARM

12290 Daffodil Lane
Unionville, VA 22567

[blueberries]

19. LIBERTY MILLS FARM

9166 Liberty Mills Road
Somerset, VA 22972

[strawberries]

20. HONEY HILL ORCHARDS

30391 Catharpin Road
Mine Run, VA 22508

[apples, pears, peaches, & plums]

21. MILLER FARMS MARKET

12101 Orange Plank Road
Locust Grove, VA 22508

[strawberries, blackberries, & pumpkins]

22. SUNRISE GARDENS

114 Sunrise Lane
Brightwood, VA 22715

[beans, blackberries, blueberries, raspberries (autumn, red), & strawberries]

23. GRAVES MOUNTAIN FARM

3611 Old Blue Ridge Tpke
Syria, VA 22743

[apples]

Apple harvest festival the first 3 weeks of October

24. SAUNDERS BROTHERS

2717 Tye Brook Hwy
Piney River, VA 22964

[peaches & apples]

FALL INGREDIENT

APPLES

Apple Brown Betty Pudding with Crème Anglaise

Dean Maupin | C&O Restaurant

INGREDIENTS

2 ½ lb (about 5 c) apples, peeled, sliced and diced
12 oz or 16 slices bread (preferably brioche or challah),
    crust removed, sliced and diced
1 ½ c granulated sugar
½ t salt
1 t cinnamon
½ t nutmeg
1 ½ c raisins
2 T lemon juice
½ c molasses
½ c butter, melted
½ c water

DIRECTIONS

Preheat oven to 350° F. Grease 14 4-oz ramekins or an 8-cup baking dish.

Place apples and bread in one large bowl. Combine butter, molasses, water, lemon juice, sugar, and spices in a separate bowl. Pour this mixture evenly over apples and bread.

Pack the apple mixture into the baking dishes. Bake at 350° for one hour. Let sit for 10-15 minutes before serving. Serve hot or warm with crème anglaise.

CRÈME ANGLAISE

2 c whole milk
2 c heavy cream
1 vanilla bean, split
8 egg yolks
8 oz sugar

In heavy medium saucepan over high heat, combine milk, cream, and vanilla bean and bring to a boil. Remove from heat.

In medium bowl, whisk egg yolks and sugar until the mixture turns pale yellow and forms ribbons on the surface.

Temper the cream mixture into yolks. To do this, add the cream mixture in 3 additions, steadily whisking throughout the whole process.

Once the cream mixture is fully incorporated, pour the sauce back into the saucepan and cook over medium heat. Stir constantly to make sure the bottom doesn't scald or the eggs curdle.

Continue stirring until the mixture thickens enough to fully coat the back of your spoon and is as smooth as silk. You can also check with an instant-read thermometer—it should be at least 156° and should not exceed 180°.

Strain the custard to remove any bits that may have curdled. Cool sauce in an ice bath.

Duck Livers with Heirloom Applesauce

Tomas Rahal | MAS Tapas

INGREDIENTS

1 lb fresh duck livers*
¼ c brandy
4 whole apples
1 cinnamon stick
6 cloves
4 cardamom pods
1 ancho chili**
2 c apple cider
1 T sherry vinegar
2 c flour
1 T smoked pimenton paprika
Sea salt and freshly ground pepper, to taste
Olive oil or duck fat

NOTES

*If duck livers cannot be found, substitute chicken livers.

**An ancho chili is very dark brown or red and is essentially a dried poblano pepper. It can be found in either the international food section or the dried bulk section of your local grocery store.

DIRECTIONS

Preheat oven to 350° F.

Clean livers in cold, salted water; trim fat and any blood vessels from exterior. Splash with brandy, season with salt and pepper, and allow to cure in the fridge for about an hour.

Toast cinnamon, clove, cardamom, and ancho chili for 10 minutes in the oven. Grind in a mortar & pestle or spice grinder.

Peel and quarter apples and place in a saucepan. Cover with cider, sherry vinegar, spices (except for the pimenton), and pinch of sea salt. Slowly simmer for about 45 minutes or until totally soft and most of the cider has evaporated. Pass through a food mill or sturdy sieve.

Heat olive oil in a skillet over medium-high heat. Dredge livers in flour seasoned with sea salt, black pepper, and pimenton. Shake off excess flour and carefully place livers in the hot oil and fry each side approximately for 2 minutes until golden brown. Remove and drain on paper towels.

To serve, spread a heaping tablespoon of applesauce on the plate. Place fried livers on top, and garnish with cracklings if you have them, or scallions cut paper-thin.

Pour a glass of Reserva Pedro Ximenez sherry (we like Toro Albala) or a rich Oloroso Sherry like Faroen from Gonzalez y Byass. Enjoy the fruits of your labor—buen provecho!

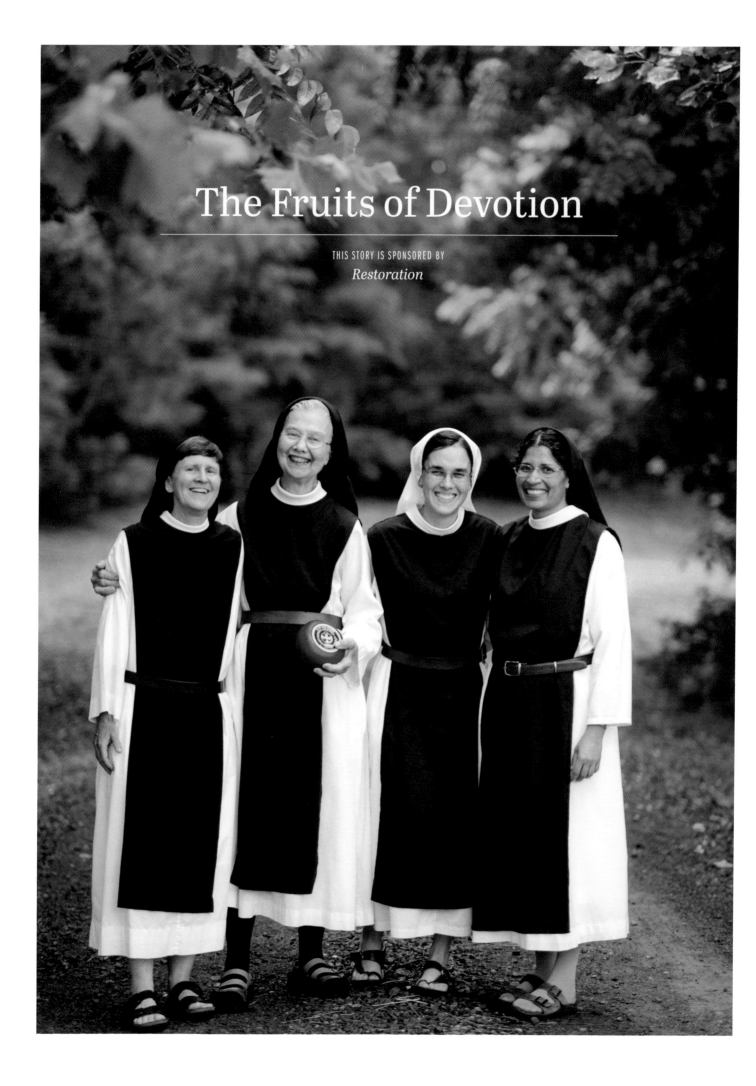

The Fruits of Devotion

THIS STORY IS SPONSORED BY

Restoration

RICHARD RIDGE HAS A BIG DAY AHEAD. HIS NEW RESTAURANT, RESTORATION, IS ABOUT TO HOST ITS FIRST DINNER SERVICE, AND HIS DAY WILL BE SPENT PREPARING FOR THE BIG NIGHT. ONE ITEM ON THE MENU IS A PLATE FEATURING SEVERAL VARIETIES OF CHEESE, INCLUDING LOCALLY SOURCED OFFERINGS, ONE OF WHICH HE NEEDS TO GO PICK UP.

Luckily, the creamery is nearby, but as he heads out in his car, his mind is running through everything that has yet to be done, as well as larger questions. What if no one shows up? What if too many people show up? What else should he do to make tonight a success?

Restoration, the restaurant venture that leads Rich up the mountain to the monastery this morning, is a partnership among Rich and Kelley Tripp, as well as Andrew Watson, owner of The Corner favorites Mellow Mushroom and Boylan Heights, among other ventures. The restaurant is located by Old Trail Golf Club in Crozet, a public golf course, and in conceptualizing it, the team has focused on considering the type of eatery that would most benefit the Crozet community. The very name itself seeks to embody a place where people can come— while playing golf, with their families, on a date night, or for a special event—and have a truly relaxing, restorative experience.

Hundreds of hours of careful thought, conversation, consideration, and labor have built up to this day, and Rich is deep in thought as he drives up the winding road outside of town this morning, toward the brick monastery where he will pick up a wheel of gouda cheese crafted by Trappist nuns who live there. As he approaches the monastery, he is struck by how peaceful it seems, tucked amid the hills and mountains. He parks his car and strides up to the door, where he is greeted by a bell and a sign that reads, "Door is open. You are welcome." He rings the bell, and a few moments later, a nun appears.

◆ ◆ ◆

The sisters of Our Lady of Angels monastery outside of Crozet, Virginia, have been making gouda cheese for twenty-three years. Founded in 1987, the monastery is home to fourteen nuns ranging in age from thirty-five to eight-two, and all are involved in the cheesemaking process, which yields 20,000 pounds a year that they sell at the monastery and through the mail. The proceeds from the cheesemaking operation are the sisters' livelihood.

"It's our tradition to earn our own living," Sister Barbara tells us when we visit the monastery on a hot late-spring day. "We always look for something on our property that might promise a future means of self-support," she says.

When the first six sisters came to live on this land in 1987, they chose the site in part for its natural beauty and seclusion. The former owner had a small cheesemaking business, creating large wheels of cheese sold wholesale. Though the nuns had no cheesemaking experience, they saw an opportunity to create a means of income. In November 1990, after they moved

into the newly completed monastery, they launched their own cheesemaking operation. Shortly after they began making cheese, *The Washington Post* caught wind of the operation. Its food editor was looking for a unique story of Virginia-crafted food, and she found it. The sisters soon found themselves on the front page of the Post's Food section, and hundreds of new customers followed.

Each batch of Monastery Country Cheese requires about 725 gallons of pasteurized milk, which results in between 330 and 370 two-pound wheels of cheese. The process takes a week from start to finish, and the sisters make 32 batches a year. About twenty percent of the cheese is sold locally, Sister Barbara estimates, with the rest selling through mail orders. And all of this has been accomplished without the sisters pursuing advertising.

"The cheese sells itself," Sister Barbara says, adding that currently they sell all they can make, and often sell out completely before Christmas.

"We only make what we need to support ourselves," she says. "We are not out to get bigger and bigger every year. It is in the service of this life we are living, and our means of self-support. We are just fortunate that it found its niche, and it has grown."

◆ ◆ ◆

When Rich reflects on that first day of picking up cheese for the restaurant, what stays with him is the immediate sense of peace he felt throughout the transaction—walking up the flower-bordered path to the door, ringing the bell, talking with the sister who helped him, exchanging money and receiving cheese in return. "It was just one of these things, it was immediately grounding; it immediately takes you down a few notches, lets you know, 'It's going to be OK'," he recalls.

Now, months after launching Restoration, Rich still makes the trip to the monastery every couple of weeks. When he visited the cheesemaking facilities not long ago, he found himself observing with keen interest how smoothly the sisters' kitchen operates. And as he watched the cheesemaking process, a word kept popping into his head: *devotion*.

"I thought about religious devotion, and then devotion to work," he says. "I know the devotion my work requires, and how it's based in love and I reach certain heights through it. Then there is the devotion that they show through their spiritual life, but also the devotion that their work requires."

He pauses, thinking of a way to sum up the exhilarating experience of launching a restaurant, and the nun's success supporting themselves, both of which are made possible by hard work and the embrace of the community.

"It's the fruits that devotion yields," he says, simply. ◆

FOR THE LOVE OF MUSHROOMS

by Brett Batten Baker

Before I was married, my culinary knowledge was, well, limited. I knew: 1) take Pop-Tart out of wrapper 2) put Pop-Tart in toaster 3) watch Pop-Tart in toaster and make sure it doesn't get burnt, just browned. I'm kidding, kind of. I also knew how to make microwave popcorn.

Moving to Charlottesville was a real-eye opener. You mean locally owned, grown, and operated wasn't just something you read about in *Little House on the Prairie?* All I knew was all of my cool Cville friends kept saying "local" and I for darn sure didn't want to be left out of something cool. I signed up for my first vegetable and fruit share. And to be honest, it was more for solidarity's sake than for my palette's. I toted around my little canvas bag and left with strawberries that felt soft and juicy, and by golly, they were actually *red* on the inside. I learned what a leek was, and I made a prosciutto, potato, and leek stew that very night—and for three nights after that, too.

I was insatiable. Charlottesville had created a Localvore. I had my first "local" restaurant meal at, well, The Local, which is where I met the second love of my life: the a.m. Fog oyster mushroom, as a part of the mushroom ragout dish. Soon thereafter, I met up with another a.m. Fog mushroom, the shiitake, on Blue Mountain Brewery's a.m. Fog Burger and have been to either one of those restaurant locations for one of those meals for every birthday, Mother's Day, anniversary or available evening (I exaggerate) since. Every mushroom I'd met until this point had tasted the exact same to me: like a mushroom, sometimes a tad heavy on the "mush." But these are different, y'all. Real different. The shiitake is meaty and has a bit of tang. The oyster is a little bit lighter, refreshing even. I'm drooling. And cooked in truffle oil? I swoon.

I used to see eating as a means of satisfying hunger. Now, it's an experience. I enjoy eating the way some enjoy going to movies or hiking trails. I used to see cooking as something that made dirty dishes. Now, I see it as an experiment or a challenge. What can I do to make this dish better? I enjoy cooking the way some enjoy painting or making music.

A far cry from microwave popcorn, huh? ◆

LAIRD & COMPANY
D.S.P. VA-5
R.C. 53G
O.P. 130
APPLE BRANDY
06L20-
08J09-
06L30-
07K26-

Cider's New Frontier

In a storeroom in Free Union, Virginia, wooden barrels are stacked on a rack reaching the ceiling, holding cider that has been aging for between four and eight months. Before cider, they aged apple brandy and before that, bourbon. If you've never thought of of cider being aged in brandy barrels before, for Tim Edmond and Dan Potter, that's the idea.

Co-creators and co-owners of Potter's Craft Cider, Dan and Tim have been producing cider since 2010. After meeting at Princeton, they each pursued careers in their respective fields—finance for Tim and engineering for Dan. They stayed in touch and found themselves enamored with agriculture and craft ale, and less enamored with their career paths. On a whim, Dan created a small test batch of traditional cider, and it was a hit. "I'd never tasted anything like it," Tim says. "I'd never had a dry cider before made with real apples and no sugar."

Until a few years ago, traditional cider was hard to come by in the United States. While cidermaking goes back centuries, the craft had fallen by the wayside in this country. With the notion that they might be onto something, Dan and Tim left their careers and started Potter's Craft, eventually landing at this spot in Free Union, a converted former horse veterinarian clinic amid the rolling hills northwest of Charlottesville. From here they have made their Farmhouse Dry cider a local darling, sold in sixty establishments around Charlottesville and nearly twenty in Richmond.

Last year, Dan and Tim got the idea to try to oak-barrel age their cider. While this method had gained some popularity among craft beer makers, it hadn't been done in the world of contemporary cidermaking. When considering the type of barrels to use, Dan and Tim thought it would be ideal to find barrels that had been used in the creation of apple-derived liquor. Thus, to oak-barrel age their cider, the duo have used thirty-six barrels sourced from Laird & Company, the oldest continually operating distillery in the country, which specializes in apple brandy and applejack. To produce its brandy, Laird uses charred white oak barrels that previously aged bourbon for up to twelve years. Depending on the type of brandy Laird is making, the barrels will then age brandy for up to another twelve years. So, some of these barrels may have spent more than two decades aging liquor before they arrive at Potter's Craft Cider.

The barrel aging adds caramel, vanilla, and brandied cherry notes to the cider,

as well as a toasted flavor imparted from the oak. The result is Potter Craft Cider's Oak Barrel Reserve. The ability to take a centuries-old tradition and try something completely new is exactly what prompted Dan and Tim to launch Potters Craft in the first place.

"It's like the Wild West," Tim says, of the country's nascent contemporary cider industry. "There's not a book that tells you how to do it: you have to experiment. That's the fun for us. It's an adventure."

In a pasture next to the storeroom, Tim and Dan have planted eighteen heir-loom apple trees known for adding tannic flavor to traditional cider: Goldrush, Harrison, and Hughes' Crab, the latter of which was grown at Thomas Jefferson's Monticello. Dan and Tim make a point of sourcing their apples from Virginia, namely Nelson County, Harrisonburg and the Shenandoah Valley, but tannic apples like these are difficult to come by. In four to five years, when these trees start to bear fruit, this small orchard will lend its history to Potter's Craft Cider, helping it to plant deeper roots, and grow. ◆

CRAFT CIDER: ROOTS AND REVIVAL

by Tim Edmond | Co-Owner, Potter's Craft Cider

Craft cider may seem like a new trend, but the art of cider making and the history of cider drinking goes back centuries. Today's hard cider resurgence is a revival of what was an early American reality. With settlers fearing the consumption of local water, which was often unsafe or unpleasant to drink, most opted for either milk or alcoholic beverages as a substitute. Without the resources to import ale or wine from abroad, making good booze at home quickly became a colonial mandate. Early attempts at growing barley and hops in New England proved unsuccessful. Apple trees, however, could be grown almost anywhere in the Colonies, and the bounty of fruit that each tree produced gave the colonists enough apples to eat, trade, and even store. Better still, when pressed into juice and fermented, they would keep far beyond the winter months and into seasons ahead. Alcohol acted as a preservative, and the nutrients of the apples were kept intact in the fermented "hard" cider.

By 1775, one out of every ten farms in New England owned and operated a cider mill, and cider was quickly becoming the national drink of choice. Cider was readily available to most early settlers, and in rural areas it was even used as currency. It was cheap, plentiful, and consumed voraciously by farmers and statesmen alike. As noted by Ben Watson in *Cider, Hard and Sweet*, it has been estimated that in 1767, the per capita average consumption of hard cider in New England was 1.14 barrels per person (25). This represents approximately thirty-five gallons of cider per person across every member of the New England society. Many early thinkers (epic drinkers) became champions of cider and its apparent health benefits. Watson notes that John Adams attributed a "tankard of cider every morning" to his good health, and Lazarus Redstreak wrote in 1801, "Experience shows that the use of cider consists with sound, healthy, and long life" (25).

As cider developed widespread popularity in the United States, it came up against its fair share of opposition in the temperance movement. As Prohibition came into full swing in the early 1920s, cider was a prime target. In addition to banning its production, sale, and consumption, cider's opponents targeted its very source. Many orchards at that time produced apple varieties that were particularly well suited to cider production but less favorable for eating. These apples were tart, tannic, and might have tasted bitter, but they made excellent cider and the temperance activists knew it. Some orchards were burned down while others were dug up, usually in favor of crops that had better commercial value during Prohibition.

Simultaneously, the U.S. population was changing. Immigrants from Europe, particularly Germany, were bringing with them a penchant for beer. When Prohibition was repealed, cider suffered a perfect storm. In addition to the lack of suitable cider apples, barley—which had alternate uses throughout Prohibition—was available immediately following the law's repeal. Barley was portable, it kept well, and it could be transported into cities and population centers to make beer. To replant apple trees would take four to five years, which would have been a really long time to wait for a drink. During this time, the nation all but forgot about cider, and its sales plummeted.

In the past ten years, cider has begun to make a comeback. Even still, in 2012, cider sales only account for approximately 0.3 percent of the domestic beer market. In similarly apple-rich countries—such as the United Kingdom—that did not undergo a period of Prohibition, cider accounted for roughly 17 percent of the beer market. Despite the relatively small size of the cider market in the United States, the category is growing rapidly, with an estimated 100 percent sales increase between 2011 and 2012.

For the most part, the resurgence of hard cider in the United States is being driven by a handful of large producers; however, similar to recent trends in craft beer, small craft cider producers are popping up in large numbers and they are taking the drink to another level. Long-forgotten apple varieties are being revived and adding serious flavor, aroma, acidity and tannin—staples of good cider. Above all, and most excitingly, there aren't yet "industry norms" in hard cider making. There are hundreds of apple varieties growing across the country, the characters of which differ dramatically, and it is up to the producers to define what is to become of the cider category in the United States. Who will drink cider? What types of apples will be used? Will it be consumed as a substitute for beer or wine, or as its own category all together? These questions and many others are being answered as the industry becomes more robust, more producers create new varieties of ciders, and apple-producing regions develop unique cider styles and their own distinct terroir.

While cider laid deep roots in early American history, the story feels like it is still at its beginning. When you plant an apple seed from any given apple, you do not know what kind of tree will grow. But with the right care and attention, and with enough seeds (think Johnny Appleseed), you end up with incredible diversity. With so many new cideries springing up in apple-producing regions across the country, the quality and diversity of ciders being produced is getting better every year, as producers continue to innovate with a thirst and passion for quality cider. ◆

BOOKS REFERENCED IN THIS ESSAY

"Cider, Hard and Sweet: History, Traditions, and Making Your Own," by Ben Watson. Woodstock: Countryman Press, 1999.

OCTOBER 22

by Lindsey Hepler

Sunlight streams in through the blinds as I roll over, half asleep. Realizing it is Saturday morning, and I am suddenly wide awake, excited for a beautiful fall day and another trip to the market. I quietly leave the bedroom, grab my market basket, and head out. From April to December, you can find me at the City Market on Saturday mornings. These weekly visits, alone or with friends, have become a highlight of my week—moments I cherish and look forward to.

As I step outside to begin the short walk to the market, crisp autumn air greets me and I marvel at the beauty of my town. Crossing the Downtown Mall, I think, *I love this place.*

My excitement builds as I enter the market. The first stop is always the same: Shenandoah Joe's for coffee. They feature two or three of their many coffee varieties each week, and I discuss the options with the barista, debating which to try today.

Meandering past stalls of orchids, cheeses, baked goods, and produce, my next stop is Appalachia Star Farm, where I pick up my tenth and final CSA share. Each week, I am presented with a new cast of vegetables. Last week the share included kohlrabi; today, turnips. The CSA has pushed me to explore the endless array of vegetables that grow in our region throughout the year. Walking away today is bittersweet—I'll have to wait until next spring to once again enjoy weekly shares of fresh, new, and exciting vegetables.

Continuing along, I buy eggs from Free Union Grass Farm and late-season raspberries from Radical Roots. Raspberries are my favorite fruit, so I am excited by this one final appearance. Even the honey stand, Bees 'n Blossoms, offers new foods to sample—this time in the form of whipped honey.

I have saved the best for last: kombucha. Although I brew my own at home, Nugget's Raw Kombucha produces a range of creative flavors too complex to make for myself. Today I purchase a bottle of Citra Hops, a tart blend of grapefruit and hops.

The only downside to my market visit is the limitation of my own two hands. Attempting to balance two heavy bags, a cup of coffee, and a camera, I make my way home. Back at my apartment, meal plans form in my head as I put away my purchases. I imagine roasted chicken and vegetables; pasta with braised greens and sausage; goat cheese and arugula salads. And what to do with those turnips?

With everything in its proper place, I sit down for breakfast featuring a scone, raspberries, and a drizzle of honey atop a bowl of yogurt. Eating this meal, made from local foods, by people I call *friends*, I marvel at these simple pleasures. With my next bite, the berries and honey taste just a bit sweeter.

These weekly trips to the market ground me. There is something so satisfying in knowing the soil and the hands that have produced my food. This community, the amazing individuals I meet at our market, makes this place *home*. ◆

THE MARKET

by Annie Runkle

The colors are brilliant
earth's bounty displayed
our fair city's market
a must-stop Saturdays

The seasonal harvest
arranged with great care
greens, roots, berries, herbs,
eggs, meat—all found there

Among those who grow
the artistes set up shop
sharing their soul-work
to wear, sip, eat up

Finding goods for the week
an inspiring rite
to check off the stock list
to add in new delights

Every spring they return
like birds from migration
for Charlottesville dwellers
a grand celebration!

ALL I REALLY NEED TO KNOW, I LEARNED FROM PASTRIES

by Alex Peterson

Our kitchen does not look like a classroom but it serves me as such. Dishes float in sudsy water beneath an open window, country music plays on the radio, and on the floor are scattered pieces of broken candies and rivers of dried food coloring. Sitting on my stool in that strange classroom, I've learned countless lessons. From that stool, I've spent hours in a haze of Zen-like wonder watching my mom turn butter and flour into edible masterpieces.

Thornton Wilder said, "My advice to you is not to inquire why or whither, but just enjoy your ice cream while it's on your plate—that's my philosophy." Such a philosophy is akin to one my mom also lives by. To truly enjoy that post-dinner treat, one has to be consumed by the moment and savor each bite. Decadence is about the process. If desserts teach us something about life, than they teach us the key to a decadent life is remembering we are constantly in the process of reaching that place. To indulge in a dessert does not mean to indulge in immediate satisfaction. The process is a much slower one. To properly eat dessert one must take in the moment, maybe even close the eyes and feel the ability to truly appreciate something.

A dessert teaches a person to savor time, to live in the moment, to welcome, and to remember that for some moment in life, however brief, many of us have been blessed with experiencing happiness. My mom doesn't simply make desserts as a job. With each sheet of fondant she rolls out and with each sugar granule she converts to caramel, she does something much more. She reminds people to stop and take a minute to acknowledge what lies in front of them. Her ability also exists as a gift to her clients, her children, her friends, and anyone who takes enough time to get lost in sugar.

Mom can take us back to younger days when satisfaction wasn't ruined by the thought of a burgeoning waistline. A warm chocolate chip cookie used to be able to make an entire day the best day ever. In that cozy kitchen where I've spent the last six years of my life, my mom manages to keep that feeling alive. You can see love and lust dancing out of the crumbs of a tart; from the steam of an apple pie bursts glorious warmth. She often has flour streaked across her face and her feet are sore constantly from standing all day, but when someone shares her love of simple happiness, she beams. ◆

SWEET POTATOES

Curried Sweet Potato Soup

Gail Hobbs-Page | Caromont Farm

INGREDIENTS

3 lbs sweet potatoes, peeled and cut into 2-inch chunks
1 medium Vidalia onion, or any sweet onion such as Maui, chopped into 2-inch chunks
1 leek, white part only, washed and chopped uniformly
2 shallots, chopped uniformly
3 T butter
1 ½ T garam masala
1 ½ t vindaloo curry powder
1 ½ t cinnamon
1 ½ t minced fresh ginger (you may substitute ground ginger)
1 bay leaf (don't lose them!)
white peppercorns, freshly ground
1 qt. chicken stock
salt, to taste
dash of honey and orange zest to finish (optional)
1 pt. shiitake mushrooms, stems removed and sliced very thin
a sprig or two of fresh thyme
8 oz. crème fraîche
3 oz. Caromont Farm fresh chèvre

DIRECTIONS

Melt butter in a large Dutch oven over low heat. Add onions, leeks, shallots, and squash. Cover and slowly sweat on low heat until squash is done and all "aromatics" are fork-tender, about 25 minutes.

Add spices and stir until vegetables evenly coated. Add the chicken stock and increase heat until soup reaches a slow boil, then reduce heat to low. Cover and simmer for about 30 minutes, or until vegetables are extremely tender.

In the meantime, in a food processor, combine crème fraîche and Caromont chèvre until just incorporated, about 10 seconds. Do not mix for long or the cream will break. Set aside for garnish.

To prepare the mushrooms, preheat the oven to 500° F. Place a nonaluminum baking sheet in the oven and let it sit until very, very hot. Pull the oven rack out and toss the mushrooms on the hot sheet pan. You will hear the mushrooms sizzle. Cook for two minutes and then pull them out. Season with fresh thyme leaves, sea salt, and freshly ground white pepper. Set aside.

Once the soup is done, drain the solid mass from the soup mixture, separating liquid with a fine mesh strainer. Reserve liquid.

Purée the curried vegetables in a blender. Be sure to take out the bay leaf! If too thick, add the cooking liquid until you've reached desired consistency. Once finished, transfer the soup to a clean saucepan and heat to proper temperature. Add more cooking liquid if needed.

Adjust seasonings: salt and white pepper, honey, and finely grated orange peel, all to taste.

Warm bowls and distribute hot soup between them. Place seared mushrooms in center of the bowl. Place one dollop of the chèvre crème in the center and allow it to melt into the hot soup. Garnish with cilantro.

Curried Quinoa Salad with Roasted Sweet Potatoes, Currants, and Mint

Amalia Scatena | Pippin Hill

INGREDIENTS

1 c dried quinoa
1½ c water or chicken stock
1 T extra virgin olive oil
2 sweet potatoes
1 T curry powder
½ c dried currants
¼ c chopped fresh mint
1 lime
2 shallots, minced
1 carrot, diced small
1 t kosher salt
½ t black pepper

DIRECTIONS

Place sweet potatoes on a lightly oiled baking sheet. Using a paring knife, make 4 small incisions to allow steam to escape potato while baking. Bake the potatoes in a preheated 350° F oven for 45 minutes, or until soft enough to put a knife all the way through. Peel the sweet potatoes while they are still warm and chop into bite-sized pieces.

Mix extra virgin olive oil and curry powder in a 1–2 quart saucepan and heat over medium heat to toast the curry to a light paste for 2–3 minutes. Add in the stock or water, salt, pepper and quinoa. Bring to a boil. Cover, reduce heat and simmer for 20 minutes, or until the liquid has been absorbed. Remove from the heat and place in a bowl. Add all other ingredients, including the sweet potatoes, and fluff gently with a fork.

Adjust seasoning if more salt and pepper is needed. Add lime zest and juice to taste, to bring out the richness of the flavors.

Can be served hot as a side dish or cold as a wonderful salad, taken on a picnic with a great bottle of Chardonnay.

Downhome Ham

THIS STORY IS SPONSORED BY
Revolutionary Soup + The Whiskey Jar

Will Richey proudly dubs himself a "ham geek." He comes by it honestly. His grandfather was an avid lover of Virginia foods, like Chincoteague oysters and, of course, cured ham. On that front, he was brand loyal.

"My grandfather was a big Kite's Ham fan," Will explains. "And so growing up, that's what we had—Kite's Ham. That's all we were served; that's all we heard about: Kite's Ham."

Chef and owner of local lunch hub Revolutionary Soup and Southern food favorite The Whiskey Jar, both on the Downtown Mall in Charlottesville, Will found his way to the culinary world through the wine business. A fascination with French wine led to an adoration of French food; in each case, he was especially taken by how different regions, and even villages, produced products with unique flavors.

This made Will wonder what his Virginian food roots were, a path that led back squarely to his grandfather, and Virginia ham. Will started working with country ham at Revolutionary Soup, where he would get a Virginia ham, remove the bone, and then slice it thinly, like prosciutto, and put it on salads, sandwiches, and traditional prosciutto-melon balls.

"To me, a Virginia ham is aged like prosciutto, it is treated like prosciutto, it should be served like prosciutto," Will says.

"I hate calling it prosciutto," he adds later. "I wish there was a word for thinly sliced Virginia ham."

When he launched The Whiskey Jar in early 2012, Virginia ham went from a personal interest to a staple product in his restaurants. "Virginia ham is one of our biggest culinary heritages," Will explains, discussing the prevalence of Virginia ham on The Whiskey Jar's menu. "I wanted this place to be an outlet for Virginia foodways and Virginia food products, so I'm trying to do everything with ham that I can."

By this time, Will was raising his own pigs at his family's Red Row Farm, and sending his own ham to Kite's, his grandfather's favorite, located just south of Madison, Virginia, for curing. Zach Miller at Timbercreek Farm was doing the same.

"When the product started showing up, and we got to taste it, we were blown away. It was tremendous," Will recalls of tasting his own homegrown pork after it was cured by Kite's. He loves the subtleties, which he feels is often lost in Virginia hams processed by larger outfits. "It's simple— they're not doing anything fussy," he says of Kite's curing process. "But to me, it's a better, more complex flavor than a lot of the other Virginia hams."

Rodney Shelton, manager at Kite's, feels it is the brown sugar content that gives

Kite's hams a unique taste. "A lot of people say 'sugar-cured' but they don't use as much brown sugar as we do," he explains, adding that they have a specific amount that they add per 100 pounds of salt. The cure consists of salt, brown sugar, and pepper.

Kite's is a six-person operation, started by Jim Kite in the 1960s. Jim was a minor league baseball player; he started the initial ham business as an off-season pastime. Once he retired from the minor leagues, he began to cure ham full time, producing around 400 finished hams a year. That number is now 18,000, and Jim, who is now eighty-one years old, remains an integral part of the six-member team that constitutes the entire operation at Kite's.

pany's customers are folks like Will or Zach, who bring in their own slaughterhouse-processed ham to have cured. For folks like these, who often raise their ham using organic or natural methods, Kite's has a slightly different curing recipe, one that does not include sodium nitrate. The rest of Kite's business is made up of the cured hams, or hams it then cooks and processes further to create products used by customers like grocery store delis. As with many specialty food producers, Rodney estimates that about half of the hams Kite's sells in a year are sold in the three months preceding Christmas.

Kite's is a very locally focused business, with most of its customers within a 100-mile radius of the warehouse. The

---

"It's a very small-business feel. It feels like they're really taking a hands-on, artisan approach."

The curing process takes two days per pound, so a forty-pound ham cures for about eighty days in a cooled environment. About 1,800 to 2,000 hams are cured at a time in the operation's sole curing warehouse. After this, they hang for about eighteen days in an environment heated to eighty-five degrees Fahrenheit, as they lose about 18 percent of their original weight, the figure dictated by the USDA before a ham cured this way can be sold. From start to finish, the entire process can take about four months.

Rodney, who took a part-time job at Kite's his first day after high school graduation and is now a part-owner of the business, estimates that about ten percent of the com-

company delivers to its customers on Tuesdays, with a 400-mile delivery route that goes as far south as Roanoke and as far north as Edinburg.

This is part of the appeal for Will. "It's a very small-business feel," he says. "It feels like they're really taking a hands-on, artisan approach." The fact that he's now a regular customer of his grandfather's favorite ham curing company is not lost on Will. In fact, for him, that's the point.

"We're raising Virginia pigs organically, the way that our grandparents would have been doing it," he says. "And they are being cured in the method that they would have been curing them, right here." ◆

Tools of
the Trade

THIS STORY IS SPONSORED BY

Happy Cook

Todd Grieger is a self-proclaimed knife enthusiast. A veteran of Charlottesville's kitchens, including five years as head chef at Maya, he is now a line cook at Glass Haus Kitchen, where he's been since its opening in November 2012.

"We try to make food better with texture," he explains of the restaurant's so-called "inspired American" cuisine. "Manipulating texture is the way of changing food these days, I think—changing the mouthfeel. The flavors are done in a different way, taste different, because you can put different things together."

the lessons one by one. He eventually landed a cooking gig at Downtown Grille. His career since has encompassed positions including general manager, sous chef, and head chef in many of the town's flagship establishments, like Blue Light Grill and C&O Restaurant, among others. Each place helped Todd broaden his skill set through experience.

At Blue Light, Todd worked for Mike Ketola, another longtime fixture of the Charlottesville restaurant scene. Mike has been the sous chef at Mas Tapas for eight years. A native of Minnesota, his family

---

"You've got to use it all day, so it's got to be comfortable."

Key to creating this variance in texture is precise knifework. And key to that, in Todd's mind, is a high-quality knife. Todd is a devotee of Japanese knives, which he loves for the hard steel—allowing for a sharper blade—as well as the ergonomic handle.

"You've got to use it all day, so it's got to be comfortable," he says.

A Charlottesville native, his early restaurant career included a stint as a server, but he quickly discovered he had an interest in cooking, so he bought Jacques Pépin's *La Technique* and worked through

moved to Virginia while Mike was in grade school. After high school, he attended James Madison University for a year on a physics scholarship, but the college path wasn't a good fit. He took a job cooking at a fast food restaurant, then quickly graduated to a steakhouse. A couple of years later, he moved down to Charlottesville and began working in the city's food scene in places like Rococo's, Blue Light, Star Hill Brewery, Jarman's Gap Restaurant (now Three Notch'd Grill), Michael's Bistro, Bodo's Bagels, and Mellow Mushroom.

Both Todd and Mike have honed their skills through the nomadic professional path common in the culinary world; neither had a formal culinary education. Charlottesville's culinary community offers a vast array of cuisines, methods, and approaches for professionals like Todd and Mike. Charlottesville's locally owned dining establishments each seek out a niche, and while there is a healthy dose of competition, there is also a heap of mutual respect and support. This is because local chefs see the importance of bolstering one another in order to ensure that Charlottesville's fine dining scene remains full of locally owned restaurants.

The same could be said for local retailers, and Todd and Mike are quick to point out the value in their careers of having a well-appointed local kitchen shop. For them, that place is The Happy Cook.

A mainstay of Charlottesville's retail community, The Happy Cook has been selling culinary supplies from its location at Barracks Road Shopping Center for thirty-five years. It already had a devoted local following when Monique Moshier and Steve Belcher purchased the store in 2005. With a lifelong interest in culinary arts, Monique took a part-time job at The Happy Cook in 2002. Three years later, she was approached by the now-former owner about buying the place.

In 2009, Monique and Steve moved the business from its original corner store-

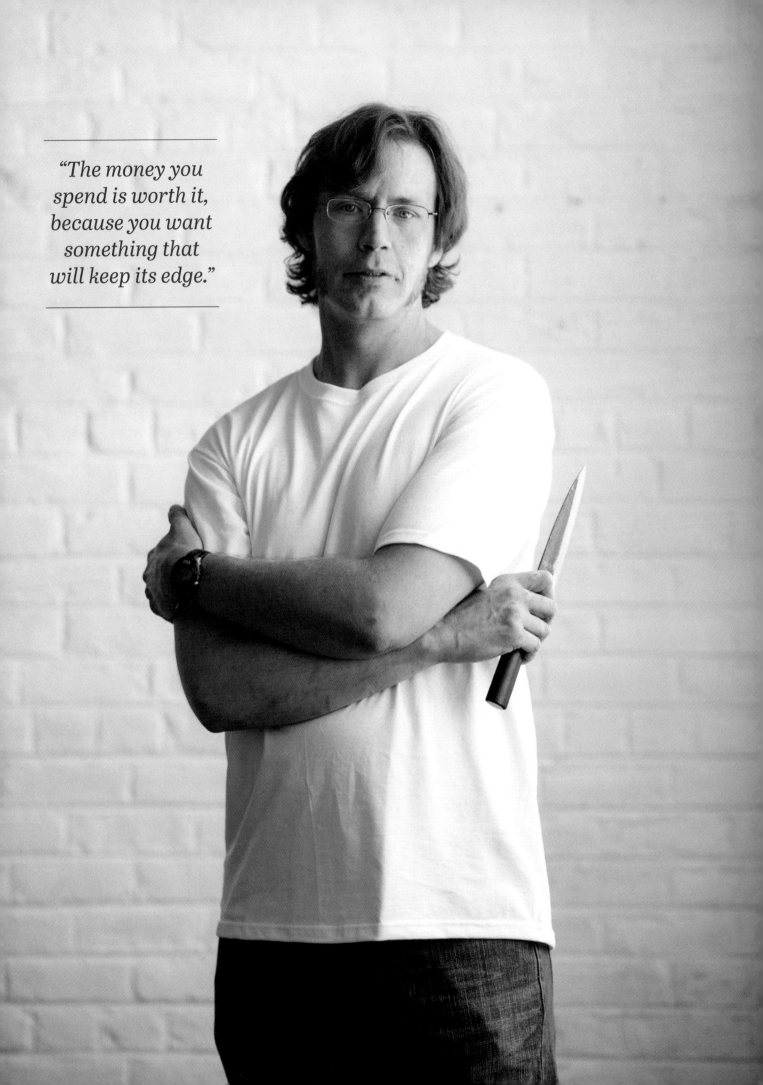

"The money you spend is worth it, because you want something that will keep its edge."

front location across the street to a larger space. This gave them the ability to deepen their inventory and in so doing, cast a wider customer net. It seems to have worked; their clientele includes everyone from folks needing a staple kitchen utensil, to culinary enthusiasts looking for something specialized, to chefs and other culinary professionals—like Todd and Mike. Their goal is to cater to all of these customers. The larger space also enabled them to begin offering cooking classes taught by area chefs on everything from cooking with locally sourced ingredients to chocolate making to knife skills.

Having a thriving, independently owned kitchen shop these days is no easy feat with competition from big box stores and high-end chains. But Monique and Steve are making it work. And in fact, they are doing better than that: The Happy Cook was recently named among the top-performing single-location independently owned kitchen shops in the country.

As with Charlottesville's independently owned restaurants, which see the value in supporting one another in order to keep the city's restaurant scene full of unique eateries, Steve feels that he and Monique's mission with The Happy Cook is not just

to convince folks to shop at a local kitchen shop because they feel they should. He aims to sell them on the shop's superior products and customer service.

"What we're trying to be—and what we hope people see that we are—is excellent," he says.

One reason people like to go to kitchen shops is the ability to examine in person the items they are seeking, comparing how each feels and looks. This is exactly how both Todd and Mike suggest shopping for a knife.

"The money you spend is worth it, because you want something that will keep its edge," Mike says. "As we all know, a sharp knife is less dangerous than a dull knife, in that you're going to make precise cuts and you can anticipate where a sharp knife is going."

Keeping a knife sharp is so important that Todd suggests it should be a primary consideration when one is shopping for a knife: a home cook needs a knife that can be easily sharpened, be it by the cook themselves or through a knife sharpening service like the one offered by The Happy Cook.

If a family or home cook is going to invest in just one knife, an eight-inch chef's knife is, in his opinion, the way to go. Knives larger than that are harder to effectively wield, especially for women or people with smaller hands. He notes that GLOBAL makes a fine line of knives for a home cook, and the brand's eight-inch chef's knife is an excellent choice.

For more advanced culinary enthusiasts, Todd adores his aforementioned Japanese knives, though reiterates that they require proper care. Hand-hewn Japanese knives require Japanese water stones in order to sharpen them correctly. In fact, Todd has a side business hand-sharpening knives for other culinary professionals.

Mike does not call himself a knife enthusiast, though it is something he has been actively learning about throughout his career. To the extent that he has developed brand loyalty, Mike has long been a fan of Wusthof Grand Prix knives, because he finds them comfortable. In fact, his advice for anyone choosing a knife—be they a casual cook or a professional—is to choose something comfortable that they feel confident they can use.

"The more comfortable you are at cooking, the better your food's going to be," he says. ◆

RECIPES ON PAGE 148

SALT OF THE EARTH

Jenny Peterson | Owner, Paradox Pastry

It was a cold but sunny Sunday in late February and I was looking for something fun to do—just something different to break the winter doldrums. I'm a huge fan of Hunter Smith's beers at Champion Brewing Company and on this day, he was tapping his Olde Salt Oyster Stout and serving up oysters on the half shell from Rappahannock River Oyster Company.

The beer was the creamiest I'd ever had and the oysters slid down in perfect tandem. I was in great company and there was college basketball on. It really doesn't get much more basic than that, but it was utter perfection.

Strange *that* memory stands out more than any other. Strange how that can be. ◆

NEW WAVE

Brian Helleberg | Chef + Owner, Fleurie

About twenty years ago, Tim Burgess and Vincent Derquenne's restaurant, Metropolitain, was the first exciting, chef-focused restaurant in Charlottesville—it was always busy and buzzing. There was always a wait list to be seated, which just added to the energy and to my appetite.

I remember ordering the seared tuna. The waiter didn't ask me how I wanted it cooked. Instead, he told me how Tim and Vincent were going to cook it and that I would like it: pristine, rare, perfectly seared, and precisely sliced—served simply with a salad. I was just starting to love seafood at the time, so it was a revelation that something from the ocean could be almost untouched by the chefs and taste so clean and look so refined. ◆

IN PURSUIT OF FOOD

by Polina Oganesyan

Gnothi seauton. This classic Greek aphorism—*know thyself* in English—was my high school's motto. Quoted countless times during my formative years there, it became an aspiration that I was always aware of and strived toward. Even as I stood with my classmates on our graduation day and knew it was just the beginning of the long journey the maxim inspires, I was confident. I had a plan and that was reassuring enough. I was to be an incoming "first year" that fall at the University of Virginia. I was excited not only to be studying at Thomas Jefferson's university, but also to be finally leaving little ol' Rhode Island—and not just for any place, but for the far-away land that is the South. Or, at least, what I thought was the South. In regards to what I was going to study, I was prompted by my love and aptitude for science and health—as well as by my family's pressure—to pursue biology and eventually apply to medical school. Diploma in hand, I thought that day, as the words *gnothi seauton* were repeated to me one last time, that I had my life all figured out.

Little did I know though that life had something wholly different in mind for me, and that I would never be the Southern Belle or stellar med school applicant I foresaw myself becoming. As a fourth year, I now reflect back on the course my life took these past few years and think of Mark Twain and his advice that every dis- enchanted youth is so quick to quote: "I have never let school interfere with my education." Although this distinction is a very real struggle many must deal with at other institutions, a UVA education, in my experience, is defined by the fact that it really does takes place in *and* outside of the classroom—a dream that Thomas Jefferson built his Academical Village upon and a guiding principle that still lives on in its students and faculty. It's a unique environment that fosters an exploration and an uncovering of what makes or doesn't make each student tick. Furthermore, it not only helps them realize those truths about themselves, but also encourages them to embrace and follow them—through the friendships they develop, professors they listen and talk to, places they travel, and countless books and articles they are assigned to read.

For me, it took a year and a half to finally realize that life was too short to waste it on something that didn't make me truly happy. After a miserable year spent taking only science courses, countless conversations with close friends and mentors, and a couple of phone calls ending with tears to my mother, I'd had enough. I was ready to finally embrace what had always brought joy into my life—food. It was the way I relieved stress, the way I procrastinated, the way I celebrated, and most importantly, the way I showed my gratitude and love for others. I allowed food to pervade all aspects of my life, except in the one way that mattered most: my future. It was that change of heart—to make my passion for food more than just a hobby, but a life's purpose—that has colored all my decisions ever since.

From that moment on, my college experience has consisted of fleshing out my passion. Not only pursuing it through all the organizations, jobs, and hobbies I take on and participate in, but also coming to realize simple truths *about* food—why I and others find it so special and why it draws so as something very special. Through stories and photos, simple truths about food are shared, illustrating for others why chefs, bakers, farmers, artisan producers, and food enthusiasts around the world do what they do and, most importantly, why they love every single moment of it.

Part of coming to "know myself" at UVA has also been about embracing my roots and coming to better understand my family, who moved to America from the former Soviet Union when I was an infant. Throughout the years, I've witnessed them

---

"Good food has the power to make all life's troubles disappear and let you just be."

---

many people into making it their life's purpose. On one hand, it's the simple *magic* of it. Despite whatever might be taking place in one's life, one bite—be it a rich chocolate cake or a juicy, ripe tomato in the peak of summer—of good food has the power to make all life's troubles disappear and let you just *be*. That moment of bliss and happiness, and the ability to inspire it in others, is why I and so many others in Charlottesville chose food as their life's purpose or passion. But also, beyond that—*beyond the flavor*—are the people and places with which we associate those certain dishes or meals. They all work together to create memories, experiences, and histories that will stay with us forever and shape who we are.

I think *that*, in particular, is what draws me to food writing and why I see it turn to the same recipes over and over again for all our special occasions and holidays. Unfortunately, this has been something that I've always looked down on them for. In my mind, they were being boring and close-minded, and I wished they would step out of the box and experiment with something new. However, knowing now what I have learned about the power of food, I've come to appreciate those dishes. It is their way of not only keeping alive those memories of their past lives, but also passing down their culture and knowledge to my cousins and me. This cake is a perfect example: it is a Russified Napoleon cake and one of my favorite desserts that will forever be a part of my family's history. ◆

RECIPES ON PAGE 149

Leap of Faith

THIS STORY IS SPONSORED BY
Brookville Restaurant

THE PAST FEW YEARS IN CHARLOTTESVILLE HAVE SEEN A BLOSSOMING OF THE LOCAL FOOD CULTURE. FARMERS' MARKETS HAVE GROWN RAPIDLY IN NUMBER AND SIZE, SMALL FARMING OPERATIONS ARE SPRINGING UP ON HILLSIDES AND IN VALLEYS, ARTISANS ARE SUCCESSFULLY MARKETING THE FRUITS OF THEIR IMAGINATIONS AND LABORS, AND THE CITY NOW HARBORS SOME 300 RESTAURANTS AT ANY GIVEN TIME.

But it wasn't always this way. Downtown Charlottesville—now home to a bustling weekly City Market and dozens of restaurants, bakeries, retail shops, and music venues—was once a sleepy neighborhood in need of revitalization. In some ways, the seeds for the vibrant downtown area we know today were sown in the mid-1990s. That is when many eateries now considered mainstays of the local food scene got their start, including Hamiltons' at First and Main and Mudhouse. It is also when Gerry Newman and his wife Millie Carson opened Albemarle Baking Co.

A native of Portland, Oregon, Gerry began a baking apprenticeship in 1981 with a Swiss master baker in Seal Beach, California. In the years that followed, he moved to the San Francisco Bay Area, worked in a variety of bakeries, and met and married Millie. The couple wanted to start a family, and had the desire to have their own business, so they began looking for a place that suited those plans. Millie grew up in Blacksburg, and the couple began looking in Virginia, where Gerry was offered a position at The Homestead resort in Hot Springs. He loved the job and the wealth of knowledge it offered. But with the impending arrival of their first child, the couple felt drawn to city life, which led them to Charlottesville and The Boar's Head Inn,

where Gerry served as pastry chef for five years, and Millie worked in the accounting department. But that dream of their own business persisted, and eventually the couple felt they had to try and see if what they imagined might work. They saw an opportunity in downtown Charlottesville.

"We were lucky," Gerry says, in his characteristically humble and honest manner. "We were there at a time when we could get in inexpensively; the new owners of the buildings were willing to take a chance on someone because they were renovating these buildings and needed to lease them; there were younger bankers downtown that were willing to loan money—things were changing. Downtown was transforming. We were in the right place at the right time."

Albemarle Baking Co. opened in November 1995 in York Place, located squarely between the Downtown Mall and Water Street. Its first winter was heavy on snow and light on staff, with just Gerry, Millie and their sole employee, Dean Maupin—now a renowned local chef working at C&O Restaurant—running the bakery, with Gerry's mother, who was visiting, helping out at the counter. When spring arrived, so did the weekly City Market in the parking lot on Water Street. Market goers started wandering into York Place and discovering Albemarle Baking Co.

"We were very fortunate," Gerry says, reflecting on how the bakery then began to develop a strong following. Soon came its initial wholesale accounts—Mudhouse, Bellair Market, and Greenberry's among them—which Gerry knew would be instrumental to the bakery's long-term success. As its commercial business grew, so did its need for space, and in 2001 Albemarle Baking Co. relocated to Main Street Market, where it was again the first commercial tenant in an up-and-coming development.

Now, eighteen years later, the bakery's retail counter hums all day long. Gerry has a staff of more than 35, including a dozen bakers, and about 130 commercial clients in the Charlottesville area including caterers, restaurants, specialty shops, and coffee shops. One of these is Brookville Restaurant, a sixty-seat affair at the end of the Downtown Mall, the vision of Jennifer and Harrison Keevil. Launched in 2010, Chef Harrison designs the restaurant's menu around fresh, seasonal ingredients, an impressive ninety percent of which are sourced locally. One of these elements from the day the restaurant opened has been Albemarle Baking Co. bread—including pain de mie, pain de campagne, olive oil rolls, butter rolls, olive and thyme bread, croissants, brioche, baguette and ciabatta—which Harrison personally chooses each day to pair with the evening's menu.

"He really cares about the craft of baking bread," Harrison says of Gerry. "He has

studied and has, in my opinion, become a master of baking bread. Plus, everyone that works at ABC are super nice; it is a pleasure to go there and pick up my bread every morning."

About a year after Brookville opened, Harrison was invited to cook in the Cochon 555 Heritage BBQ Competition in Memphis. He solicited help for the event on Facebook, and Gerry was the first person to volunteer. Albemarle Baking Co. provided bread to the event, and Gerry rode down to Memphis in an RV with Harrison, Jennifer, and a handful of other young cooks to compete in the event, cooking up Cuban pork sandwiches. Through the course of working side by side that weekend, they became friends.

"I really admire them," Gerry says of Harrison and Jennifer and the work they are doing to make Brookville Restaurant a truly local eatery in every sense of the word. A grin spreads over his face; its source is genuine and its effect contagious. Their tenacity reminds him of another couple he knew nearly 20 years ago—he and Millie.

"It's a huge leap of faith," he says, reflecting on his journey, and what he sees in Harrison and Jennifer. "You're out there, you are laying yourself bare, and you're saying, 'I'm going to do *this*. And I'm going to do it *this* way. And if it succeeds, well then, that's great. And if it doesn't succeed, I can walk away and say, 'I did it the way I thought it should be done.'" ◆

"*He really cares about the craft of baking bread. He has studied and has, in my opinion, become a master of baking bread.*"

Puréed Soup of Summer Onions, Fava Beans and English Peas with Coriander and Buttermilk, Dusted with Sumac

Gay Beery

A LOCAL AFFAIR, P. 26

1 bunch spring onions—whites and greens—finely chopped
1 small white onion, chopped
2–3 T olive oil
1 t garlic, chopped
1-2 T fresh ginger, chopped or puréed (Planet Earth Diversified's when in season)
1 ½ c shelled English peas
1 ½ c shelled/cleaned fava beans
1 T ground coriander
1 t ground cumin (ideally freshly toasted and ground)
3-4 c water or vegetable stock
1 good handful fresh mint and cilantro, chopped
salt and pinch of cayenne, to taste
3 T lemon juice
½–1 c buttermilk or yogurt
sumac for garnish

Shell and clean fava beans by ripping open the pods and removing the white husks. Either scrape off husk to reveal the light green bean or blanch quickly to help loosen husks before removing.

In stockpot, sauté the spring onions and white onion in olive oil over medium heat, for 5-7 minutes, until translucent. Add garlic and ginger.

Turn up heat to medium-high, add peas and favas, and sauté until heated through.

Add ground coriander, ground cumin, and vegetable stock or water (enough liquid to make a moderately loose soup).

Bring to a boil and reduce to simmer for just 3-5 minutes.

Quick chill (I use a bowl in an ice bath or immersion cooler), add chopped herbs, cayenne, and lemon juice before blending or puréeing in a food processor or blender.

Add buttermilk to reach desired consistency.

Serve in chilled bowl and garnish with sumac.

Makes about 2 quarts. Will serve 8-12 as a first course, 25-30 as an hors d'oeuvre.

Pizza of Wild Mushrooms, Pheasant Confit and Bloomsbury Cheese

Gay Beery

A LOCAL AFFAIR, P. 26

1 batch of your favorite pizza dough (using 2-2 ½ c flour as a foundation)
¼ c olive oil, total
½ lb wild mushrooms, trimmed and sliced appropriate to their size
2 cloves garlic, finely chopped
2 t fresh savory, sage, thyme, rosemary or combination thereof, chopped
½ lb duck or pheasant confit (you can buy this prepared, thank goodness, unless you've got some put up)
1 piece Caromont Farm Bloomsbury cheese (delicious super-creamy cow's milk cheese with an easy, bloomy rind)
2 T shaved/grated pecorino, reggiano or similar hard grating cheese

Preheat oven to 400° F.

Rise and punch down dough as needed to give you a relaxed product to work with. We like to stretch approximately 1-cup pieces of dough to make long, narrow slippers, but you can make them any size or shape you like.

Stretch dough into desired shape and place on lightly oiled baking sheet.

PREPARE MUSHROOMS

In medium sauté pan, heat 2 T olive oil over medium-high heat. Add mushrooms and sauté 4-6 minutes, stirring all the while, until nicely wilted. Add garlic, salt, and pepper to taste and chopped herbs (a splash of apple brandy at the end is also a very good thing).

Spread confit evenly over pizza—a little goes a long way. Distribute slightly cooled mushrooms over top, and finish by evenly covering in pinches of Bloomsbury cheese. Dust lightly with the grated hard cheese and pop into the oven.

Cook 20-25 minutes, checking and rotating pan about ⅔ of the way through, until pizza looks crisped on the bottom and nicely gooey and lightly browned on top.

Enjoy!

Chicken Liver Mousse with Ginger and Garam Masala, Served with Rhubarb-Cherry Chutney

Gay Beery

A LOCAL AFFAIR, P. 26

CHICKEN LIVER MOUSSE

¼ c butter for sautéing; ½ c softened butter to add later
¼ c shallots, chopped
1 T garlic, chopped
1-2 T garlic scapes, finely chopped
1 T fresh ginger, chopped or pureed
¼ c rhubarb, chopped (substitute Granny Smith apples if not in season)
1½ c fresh chicken livers, rinsed, cleaned of connecting membrane and patted dry
1 ½ t garam masala
¼ t cayenne
1 t salt and pepper, to taste

In medium sauté pan, heat butter over medium heat until sputtering stops. Add shallots and cook until soft, stirring all the while—about 5-7 minutes. Add garlic, scapes, ginger, and rhubarb and sauté another 2-3 minutes.

Turn heat up to medium-high and add chicken livers. Sauté, turning to cook all sides, until they are evenly golden, but still a little soft. (You do not want to cook them well, or the pâté will be coarse and grainy). Add the remaining seasonings—garam masala, cayenne, salt, and pepper—and stir until evenly coated. Check for seasoning.

Let cool for about 5 minutes; they should be still warm. Transfer chicken livers to food processor and add up to ½ cup of the softened butter and process until creamy.

Smooth pâté into a serving dish and lay plastic wrap over, pressing to seal off the surface. Chill at least 2 hours before serving. To serve, remove from refrigerator about 15 minutes prior, to soften.

Serve with buttered toasts or crackers, or a good baguette, and chutney.

Makes about 3 cups, or appetizers for 10-12 guests.

CHUTNEY

2 shallots, finely chopped

1 c rhubarb, chopped (substitute Granny Smith
  apples if not in season)

2–3 T olive or vegetable oil

1 c pitted cherries, coarsely chopped

1–2 T fresh ginger, finely chopped or puréed

1½ t garam masala

3 T honey

2 t rosé vinegar (or other light vinegar)

pinch of cayenne

salt to taste

In sauté pan, cook shallots in oil over medium
heat until wilted. Add rhubarb, cherries and
ginger and sauté for 3–4 minutes. Add remaining
ingredients and cook over medium heat until
juices cook down and mixture is a bit sticky (do
not caramelize). Check for seasonings, and serve
warm or room temp.

Roasted Duck Breast, Cauliflower Purée, Spring Vegetable Ragù, and Cherries

Harrison Keevil

ONE FARM, FIVE CHEFS, P. 36

CAULIFLOWER PURÉE

1 head cauliflower, chopped

3 c milk

salt, to taste

Place cauliflower, milk and salt in a pot. Bring
to a boil and reduce to a simmer. Simmer for
15 minutes, or until cauliflower is tender. Strain,
reserving milk. Place cauliflower in a blender
with ½ cup of the cooking liquid and blend until
smooth.

DUCK

4 duck breasts

1 T vegetable oil, for sautéing

salt and pepper, to taste

Heat pan to low-medium heat and add oil.
Season breasts and place in pan, skin side
down. Cook for 7 minutes, then flip over and
cook 3 more minutes. Remove from pan and
allow to rest 5 minutes.

VEGETABLE RAGÙ

1 c peas, blanched

1 c green beans, blanched

1 T butter

1/4 c water

Place water and butter in pan and heat until
butter melts. Add peas and green beans and
sauté over medium heat until liquid is gone. Be
careful not to heat too high too fast because you
will break the sauce.

PLATE

Place cauliflower purée on plate and top with
ragù. Slice duck and place on top of ragù.
Garnish with cherries and micro greens.

Bacon + Spring Onion Quiche

Gerry Newman

ONE FARM, FIVE CHEFS, P. 38

favorite pie dough

3 whole eggs

2 egg yolks

1 ¼ c milk

1 ¼ c cream

½ t salt

pepper, to taste

nutmeg, to taste

4 oz Meadow Creek Mountaineer cheese*

4 oz Meadow Creek Appalachian cheese*

8 oz bacon

4 oz spring onions

*Note: *Mountaineer and Appalachian are both
raw cow's milk cheeses from Meadow Creek
Dairy in Galax, Virginia. Mountaineer is similar
to Gruyère but softer. Appalachian is a cheese
of their own creation that showcases their
awesome milk! You could easily substitute
Gruyère Comté, Challerhocker, Fontina Val
d'Aosta or any nice, meltable cheddar.*

Whisk eggs, egg yolks, milk, cream, salt, pepper,
and nutmeg until light and fluffy.

Grate and mix cheeses.

Cook bacon until very crisp, preferably in a cast
iron skillet. Once finished, remove from skillet
and roughly chop strips into 1-2-inch pieces.
Pour out a bit of the bacon fat from the skillet
and cook spring onions in it until very soft. Add
bacon back into the pan.

Line 9-inch pan with pie dough, then line
dough with foil and fill with dried beans. Par-
bake dough for 25 minutes. Remove beans and
foil. If crust is still too pale, bake without foil for
a few minutes more.

Spread bacon-onion mixture on bottom of
crust and cover with cheeses. Pour custard into
shell and bake at 350° F for 30-40 minutes,
or just until center is set. If crust begins to
overbrown, wrap foil around the edges to
prevent further browning.

Roast Chicken with Pomegranate and Horseradish Glaze

Matthew Hart

ONE FARM, FIVE CHEFS, P. 40

POMEGRANATE-HORSERADISH GLAZE

2 c pomegranate molasses

1 c horseradish, prepared

1 T dijon mustard

Combine all ingredients until smooth and well
mixed.

*Note: Quarter the recipe if making just one roast
chicken, or reserve extra glaze for later.*

HORSERADISH AND POPPY SEED SLAW

2 c mayonnaise

½ c horseradish (freshly grated or prepared)

½ c malt vinegar

½ c sugar

¼ c poppy seeds

1 head red cabbage, shredded

1 medium carrot, grated

1 T kosher salt

Combine all ingredients except the salt, cabbage
and carrots until well mixed.

About an hour before serving, toss cabbage,
carrot, and salt together and place in a colander
in the sink.

When ready to serve, place the cabbage mixture
in a clean dish towel or paper towels and wring
out moisture. Toss with enough of the dressing to
lightly coat the cabbage mixture and serve.

ROASTED CHICKEN

3½ pound chicken

Salt and pepper, to taste

Pomegranate-horseradish glaze

Preheat the oven to 375° F. Truss the chicken
and season the outside and the cavity with
salt and pepper. (Optional: Insert meat
thermometer into thickest part of chicken thigh
at this point to monitor cooking.)

Place chicken in oiled roasting pan (don't oil the chicken itself, so that the glaze will stick later).

Place in the oven and roast until the chicken is about ¾ finished cooking (the internal temperature at the thickest part of the thigh should be about 150° F).

Brush chicken liberally with pomegranate and horseradish glaze. Continue cooking until interior temperature reaches around 165° F. (Optional: Broil for 1–2 minutes at end to further crisp skin and caramelize the glaze.) Do not be afraid if pomegranate glaze caramelizes and blackens.

Allow chicken to rest for around 10 minutes; carve and serve with mashed potatoes and the horseradish-poppy seed slaw.

Citizen Burger's Burger
Andy McClure

ONE FARM, FIVE CHEFS, P. 42
½ pound Timbercreek Organics ground beef
sea salt
ground black pepper
brioche bun, buttered
1 slice McClure Swiss cheese
1 thick-cut, char-grilled slice of white onion
1 piece crisp iceberg lettuce
2–3 slices tomato
garlic aioli sauce
pickle spear

We start with the best beef money can buy: Timbercreek beef, of course, delivered fresh and hand-pattied daily. We season with a little sea salt and ground black pepper and throw the half-pound burger over some serious flame. We don't add different cuts of meat, so guests can experience the original, grass-fed style of beef.

Once the burger is cooked "pink," we throw it on a hand-buttered, freshly baked brioche bun. Our buns are quite rich with eggs and butter and are baked and delivered fresh every day.

We top the burger with a thick slice of our premier local cheese, McClure Swiss, then throw on our signature "black onion"—a thick-cut, char-grilled slice of white onion. On top of this, we put some crisp iceberg, some slices of tomato, and our house garlic aioli, which is heavy on the egg and the garlic.

Last but not least, we spike the Citizen Burger with our fried beer-battered pickle spear and brand it with a finishing logo. Grab some of our hand-cut fries and a beer and you're in heaven.

The Perfect Steak
Will Richey

ONE FARM, FIVE CHEFS, P. 44
T-bone or Porterhouse steak
2 T garlic
2 T fresh rosemary
good olive oil
1 lemon
salt and pepper, to taste

[Note: This is more of a process than a recipe.]

Dry your steak off as best as you can with a paper towel. It also helps if you allow the steak to come to room temperature on the counter, which further aids in drying.

Get your grill nice and hot on one side. (You always want heat options when grilling.)

First rub the steak lightly with good olive oil. Mince up some garlic and rosemary, then rub this mixture into the meat. Grind fresh black pepper and salt evenly over both sides, making sure you salt the bone as well.

Grill the steak to medium rare using high heat for a good exterior char. Rest a few minutes before serving.

When steak is resting, drizzle with olive oil and a squeeze of fresh lemon juice.

Serve.

Double H Farm Arugula Dressed with Herbed Vinaigrette + Caromont Farm Bloomsbury Cheese
Mathew Allen

A LOCAL FEAST, P. 54
1 t dijon mustard
1 T red wine vinegar
½ c olive oil
chopped mixed herbs, to taste—such as rosemary, thyme, sage, parsley, or basil
salt and pepper, to taste

Whisk mustard and vinegar together. Slowly whisk in oil until emulsified. Add salt, pepper, and chopped herbs.

Lightly toss dressing with arugula and arrange with cheese slices on plate.

Double H Farm Cherry Tart
Mathew Allen

A LOCAL FEAST, P. 54
GRAHAM CRACKER CRUST
1 ½ c graham cracker crumbs (10–12 whole graham crackers pulsed in a food processor until finely ground)
¼ c granulated sugar
⅓ c butter, melted

CREAM CHEESE FILLING
16 oz. cream cheese, room temperature
½ c sugar
½ c milk
1 t vanilla extract
1 lb cherries, pitted and halved (for top)

MAKE GRAHAM CRACKER CRUST
Preheat oven to 375° F.

In a medium-sized bowl or food processor, combine graham crackers, sugar, and melted butter. Blend until the texture of coarse meal.

Lightly butter a 9- to 10-inch pie dish. Press graham cracker crumb mixture evenly into bottom and up the side of the pie plate, keeping the crust about ⅛ inch thick all around. Make sure there are no gaps or holes.

Note: If you chill the crust for a hour before you bake it, this will help prevent crumbling when you serve.

Bake approximately 10–12 minutes. The edges may be just slightly browned, but you do not want the edges or crust to overbrown. Remove from oven and let cool on a wire rack before filling.

MAKE FILLING
Beat sugar and cream cheese until well mixed. With mixer set on low, add milk and vanilla. Once incorporated, increase speed to medium, and beat until smooth and there are no more lumps.

Add to pie shell. Chill in the refrigerator. After about one hour, top with the halved cherries. Chill until ready to serve.

Before serving, loosen the pie crust from the pan (to ensure clean plating) by dipping the bottom in hot water for a few seconds.

Polyface Farm Roasted Chicken, Roasted Double H Farm Carrot and Summer Courgette
Mathew Allen

A LOCAL FEAST, P. 54

1 3-4 lb chicken

1 lb baby carrots

2 lb baby courgette (zucchini)

Dry chicken, season with salt, pepper, and olive oil. Add fresh thyme and rosemary to inside. Place in shallow pan in 425° F oven for 20 minutes, then reduce temp to 350° F for 20 minutes per pound. (Optional: Turn temperature back up to 425° at end for 5-7 minutes to finish crisping the skin if it's not done to your liking.)

Peel carrots and toss with salt, pepper, and oil. Roast in oven at 350° F until tender. (Optional: Roast carrots around base of chicken after initial 20 minutes so they roast in the chicken's juices.)

Wash and cut squash in half lengthwise. Season with salt, pepper, olive oil, and fresh thyme. Grill over medium heat until tender.

Beer-Braised Best of What's Around Short Rib, Wade's Mill Stone-Ground Grits, Shaved Double H Farm Carrot Slaw
Mathew Allen

A LOCAL FEAST, PAGE 54

2 lb short rib

2 bottles herbaceous beer

1 qt beef stock

1 onion

4 cloves garlic

4 stalks celery

2 lb carrots

2 c ground grits

2 T tomato paste

1 T butter

Trim excess fat on short rib; season with salt and pepper. Heat a large Dutch oven or pot over medium heat and add a few tablespoons of oil. Sear each side of the ribs until golden. Remove short ribs and add large diced onion, garlic, celery and 2 carrots (roughly chopped) and tomato paste. Cook until golden brown. Add in short rib with vegetable mix and pour beer over top. Add beef stock to cover the ribs and bring to simmer. Cover and place in 300° F oven for 3-4 hours, or until meat is tender.

Meanwhile, bring 6 cups water to boil. Pour in grits gradually and stir. Reduce heat to low and cook 15 minutes. Season with salt, pepper, and butter to taste. (Optional: Add parmesan for flavor.)

Peel remaining carrots and shave with peeler. Place in cold water in fridge until ready to use. To serve, drain from water, toss with olive oil, white wine vinegar, salt, and pepper.

Once beef is cooked, remove 2 cups of the cooking liquid and make a sauce by reducing liquid by half in a pan. Remove from heat and whisk in a tablespoon butter.

Green Tomato Pickles
Craig Hartman

VIRGINIA FOOD ROOTS, P. 60

1 ½ c cider vinegar

½ c water

3 T kosher salt

½ t black pepper

1 c sugar

3 cloves garlic

2 T pickling spice

2 lbs large green (unripe) tomatoes, diced

Mix all ingredients, except tomatoes, in a stockpot and bring to a boil, cooking until sugar and salt have dissolved.

Add green tomatoes.

Return to the stove and simmer for about 15 minutes, or until tomatoes are just starting to soften.

Remove from the stove, pour into a large tupperware container or mason jars, and refrigerate overnight.

Pear Marmalade
Provided by Leni Sorensen

VIRGINIA'S BOUNTIFUL TABLE, P. 62
Adapted from recipe by Mary Randolph, appearing in **The Virginia House-Wife** *(1824)*

Note: This recipe can make small or large quantities; allow one pound of sugar to two pounds of pears.

pears, core removed, peeled and sliced.

sugar

large saucepan for cooking pears and sugar

sieve or food mill

stockpot; sterilized jars and bands; new lids; and other water bath canning supplies

Boil pears until soft. Drain and let cool.

Once cool, process through sieve or food mill.

Add sugar. Boil until thick.

Process using water bath canning method for 20 minutes, or refrigerate immediately and enjoy within one week.

Okra Soup
Provided by Leni Sorensen

VIRGINIA'S BOUNTIFUL TABLE, P. 62
Adapted from recipe by Mary Randolph, appearing in **The Virginia House-Wife** *(1824)*

2 "double handsful" of young okra

2 onions

1 "handful" fresh lima beans

3 young patty pan squash, seeds removed and cubed

1 lb cubed chicken

½ lb bacon or pork

6 tomatoes, skin removed and chopped

1 gallon water

salt and pepper

1 T butter

1 T flour

large stockpot

Thinly slice okra on bias.

Finely chop two onions.

Add okra and onions to water in stockpot. Bring to a steady simmer; do not boil. Simmer until okra begins to tenderize.

Add fresh lima beans; let simmer until limas begin to tenderize.

Add squash; chicken or veal; bacon or pork; and tomatoes.

Let simmer 30 minutes.

Season with salt and pepper, to taste.

Melt butter in a small saucepan; add flour and whisk until the two are combined in a paste, or roux.

Add roux of butter and flour to thicken.

Serve with rice.

Malted Chocolate Cheesecake with Pretzel Crust

Abby Love Smith—Pastry Chef, Hamiltons'

THE SWEET SPOT, P. 80

PRETZEL CRUST

1 c graham cracker crumbs (from about 8 full crackers)
1 c crushed pretzels (from about 2 cups of mini pretzel twists)
⅓ c brown sugar
⅔ c melted butter

MALT CHOCOLATE FILLING

1 c malted milk powder (like Carnation brand)
1 c heavy cream
24 oz (3 8-oz packages) cream cheese, room temperature
1 ½ c sugar
¼ c flour
8 oz dark chocolate, melted
5 eggs
8 oz sour cream
1 T vanilla

GANACHE TOPPING

8 oz dark chocolate
1 c cream
¼ c malt powder

MAKE THE PRETZEL CRUST

Preheat oven to 325° F. Butter a 9- or 10-inch springform pan and wrap the outside in foil. Put a few quarts of water on to boil (to be used in water bath, later).

In a medium bowl, stir together the crumbs, crushed pretzels, and sugar. Add the melted butter and mix until evenly moistened. Press onto the bottom and up the sides of the pan. Bake until your kitchen starts to smell awesome and the crust looks a shade darker, 13–15 minutes. Leave the oven on.

MAKE THE MALT CHOCOLATE FILLING

Heat the heavy cream in a small saucepan and add the malt powder, whisking until smooth and the malt powder has fully dissolved. Set aside to cool slightly.

Cut the cream cheese into large chunks and drop into a food processor or stand mixer with the sugar. Process for 30–45 seconds, stopping to scrape down the sides with a rubber spatula at least once. Mix until the cream cheese is creamy and uniform. If mixed using a stand or hand mixer, beat the cream cheese and sugar about 90 seconds longer.

Add the malt-cream mixture, the flour, and the melted chocolate. Process for 20 seconds, until incorporated. Scrape down the sides. With the motor running, pour in the eggs one by one, allowing them to incorporate before adding the next. Stop the mixer. Add the sour cream and the vanilla. Pulse until smooth.

Pour the filling into the crust and place into a larger roasting pan. Pour the hot water (doesn't have to be boiling, just hot) in the roasting pan about halfway up the sides of the springform. Bake for 1 hour and 15 minutes, or until the edges are puffed and the center is set. Remove from the oven and lift the cheesecake out of the water bath. Cool to room temperature, and then chill in the fridge for at least 4 hours or overnight.

MAKE THE GANACHE TOPPING

Once the cheesecake is thoroughly chilled, place the chocolate in a heatproof bowl. Heat the cream to scalding, or just before it comes to a boil. Whisk in the malt powder, and then pour over the chocolate. Allow to sit for 2 minutes, and then whisk until smooth.

Release the cake from the springform and transfer to a plate. While still warm enough to be fluid, pour the ganache over the top and spread to the edges. Impress your dinner guests by letting it dribble down around the edges a little.

Chill. Slice with a hot knife and serve cold.

Tuna + Avocado

Todd Greiger

TOOLS OF THE TRADE, P. 126

1 avocado
1 lb. sushi-grade tuna
8 oz goat cheese
1 T water
4 sprigs Thai basil
1 scallion

BEETS

1 bunch baby gold beets
1 bunch baby red beets
1 bunch baby chioggia beets
½ c olive oil
½ c red wine vinegar
¼ c orange juice

WASABI VINAIGRETTE

1 T prepared wasabi*
1 pinch sugar
1 T sesame oil
¼ c rice wine vinegar
½ c olive oil
salt and pepper, to taste

*Note: *You can find wasabi powder in the international food section of your local grocery store. To make the prepared wasabi, mix equal parts wasabi powder and water.*

PREPARE BEETS

Preheat oven to 350° F. Wash beets thoroughly and cut greens. Discard or reserve for another preparation. Trim roots and discard.

Place each type of beet in its own 9-inch by 9-inch oven-safe pan. Drizzle with olive oil to coat. Mix vinegar with orange juice and divide between three pans. Roast for about 20 minutes or until beets are easily pierced with a knife.

Remove from oven and cool completely. Peel beets and slice into even slices. Reserve.

PREPARE WASABI VINAIGRETTE

Whisk all ingredients together in a small mixing bowl. Season with salt and pepper to taste.

PREPARE GOAT CHEESE

Put the cheese in a small sauté pan. Add 1 T water. Over low heat, whisk the cheese until smooth. Remove from pan and reserve on counter until ready to serve.

Prepare tuna and avocado:

Cut the avocado in half, remove seed, and scoop from peel. Cut into wedges.

Square off the tuna. Cut against the grain into long rectangles. Cut each rectangle into squares.

TO SERVE

Place a small dollop of goat cheese at the edge of the plate. Using the edge of a spoon, make a little swoosh with the goat cheese. Arrange beet slices in a random pattern on the plate. Scatter tuna slices on top of the beets. Drizzle the plate with the wasabi vinaigrette. Garnish with Thai basil leaves and scallions.

Tomato + Coconut Soup

Mike Ketola

TOOLS OF THE TRADE, P. 126

3 T extra virgin olive oil
1 medium onion, julienned
2 T minced garlic
2 T minced ginger
4 T red curry paste
2 cans (about 3 ½ c) coconut milk

3 c vegetable, chicken, or seafood stock

2–3 large tomatoes, chopped and roughly pureed until blended

¼ c soy sauce

½ c mirin

juice of 2 limes

¼ c roughly chopped cilantro

3 T minced fresh mint

Salt and pepper to taste

1 lb sliced mushrooms, julienned chicken, or peeled and deveined shrimp (optional)

Heat olive oil in a medium stock pot. Add onions and sauté over medium heat until nearly translucent. Add garlic and ginger and sauté for approximately 1 minute. Add red curry paste and, constantly stirring, sauté for another 30 seconds.

Add coconut milk, stock, tomato purée, soy sauce, mirin, and lime juice. Bring to a boil, then reduce heat to simmer. If using mushrooms, chicken or shrimp, add at this point. Simmer for 45 minutes, stirring occasionally.

Add cilantro and mint, and simmer for an additional 5 minutes. Makes about 2 quarts.

Russian Napoleon Cake

Polina Oganesyan

IN PURSUIT OF FOOD, P. 136

Essentially a French mille-feuille, this Napoleon cake has been adapted, adopted, and fully nationalized by Russians as the Russian cake. The iconic filling is a custard-based pastry cream, elevated with the addition of sweetened condensed milk. You can make your own dough for the pastry layers; my family used store-bought puff pastry growing up. In my opinion, it provides a satisfying crunch in contrast to the rich cream. It also makes assembly a cinch once you've made the filling, which can be prepared three days in advance. Once assembled, serve immediately, although refrigerated leftovers are just as delicious.

1 c sugar

3 large egg yolks

2 ½ T corn or potato starch

2 ½ T all-purpose flour

2 c milk

1 ½ c unsalted butter, softened

¾ of a 14-oz can of sweetened condensed milk

1 ½ T vanilla extract

1 package (2 sheets) all-butter puff pastry, defrosted but still cold

powdered sugar for dusting

PASTRY CREAM FILLING

In a medium heavy-bottomed saucepan, preferably with the back of a wooden spoon, combine sugar with egg yolks until eggs are well incorporated and mixture is thick and pale yellow. Add the starch and flour and mix thoroughly until you can no longer see any lumps.

In another small saucepan (or a heatproof glass measuring cup if using a microwave on high power), heat the milk to the boiling point. Stir a few tablespoons into the yolk mixture; then gradually add the remaining milk, stirring constantly.

Heat the mixture over medium heat, stirring constantly. After a minute or two, it will begin to thicken. Continue to stir, and watch for bubbling. Once you see bubbles, whisk for three additional minutes. Remove the saucepan from the heat and place into an ice bath. Coat the top of the custard with a pat of butter to prevent a film from forming as the custard cools. Let cool to room temperature.

In a large bowl, beat butter until light and fluffy. Add sweetened condensed milk and beat for another 8–10 minutes. Add cooled custard, one heaping tablespoon at a time. Add vanilla extract and beat for another 5 minutes.

PUFF PASTRY

Defrost dough according to package instructions. Preheat oven to 350° F. On a very lightly floured surface, unfold one sheet and roll it out roughly to the size of a standard 17-inch x 12-inch sheet pan. Carefully transfer dough onto a baking sheet of the same size. Repeat with the second sheet of dough. Bake both sheets for 15 minutes or until tops are golden. Allow to cool.

TO ASSEMBLE CAKE

Trim the edges of the puff pastry layers to make it more uniform. Crumble these trimmings into a bowl and set aside. Place one layer on a long rectangular serving platter. Spread a generous amount of the pastry cream over the top. Repeat with the next layer of cake and cream. Scatter the crumbs over the top and dust with powdered sugar. Serve immediately, or within the next hour.

ABOUT THE SPONSORS

JAMES LUM & MATTHEW GREENE, JM STOCK PROVISIONS & SUPPLY
stockprovisions.com

After working together at a butcher shop in Brooklyn, James and Matthew have returned to their native Virginia to launch JM Stock Provisions & Supply, a whole-animal butcher shop that will source meat from Virginia farmers and utilize nose-to-tail butchery principles to ensure as little waste as possible. James and Matthew plan to launch the shop in autumn 2013 in downtown Charlottesville.

Zach Miller of Timbercreek Organics—from which JM Stock will source some of its meat—welcomes their addition to the Charlottesville food community. "They offer us as farmers the opportunity to bring the next level of finish and polish to what we've started at Timbercreek," he says. "They are going to offer a forum where our products are more accessible and are beautifully presented."

ZACH & SARA MILLER, TIMBERCREEK ORGANICS
tcorganics.com

From their 500-acre farm just north of Charlottesville, Sara and Zach work to ensure that they provide their clients with consistent, high-quality products, including beef, pork, chicken, duck, eggs, and produce. This means taking a highly organized, planned approach to farming that belies the seemingly simple, idyllic view of the farm one can get standing and gazing out from the barn. While the system set up here finds its roots in those created by Mother Nature, the system that sustains Sara and Zach's business is intentional and precise. But this way of life is mooring for Zach, and it is something he is grateful to be able to share with his young children.

"Everything about what we do is value-driven," he says. "It's a good vehicle for imparting the values of hard work and honesty and dedication."

CODY GRANNIS, AMORE EVENTS BY CODY LLC
amoreeventsbycody.com

Cody's philosophy is that as a wedding planner, she has been entrusted with the responsibility to make a monumental day in the lives of her clients one that exceeds the couple's expectations. The ability to rely on vendors like Gay Beery at A Pimento is key to achieving that goal.

"I get personally involved with their planning and design so by the time their wedding comes around, they trust me, I trust them and we can talk and laugh and hold hands and jump up and down about their wedding," Cody says with a grin.

"I've seen it!" Gay adds, laughing.

CRAIG + DONNA HARTMAN, THE BARBEQUE EXCHANGE
bbqex.com

When Craig and his wife Donna designed The Barbeque Exchange in Gordonsville, Virginia, in 2011, they wanted to capture the vibe of a country fair—a place that feels familiar, yet removed from the daily grind.

When it comes to The Barbeque Exchange's cuisine, Craig has something even more specific in mind. "Where do people eat in our area if they are traveling here, and they want to feel like they had an experience that gives them *Virginia*?" he asks. "We want them to feel like they leave here, and they have a piece of Virginia in their heart."

SOUTHERN ENVIRONMENTAL LAW CENTER
southernenvironment.org

With a staff of nearly sixty attorneys located throughout the Southeast, SELC leverages the power of the law to protect the environment of this region, including the quality of our air and water, as well as our region's beautiful, unique, and iconic land. It does this by working with the executive, legislative, and judicial branches of government and more than 100 partner groups to shape, implement and enforce laws and policies protecting our natural resources, including ensuring clean air; protecting forests, aviary breeding grounds, and wetlands; enacting mercury pollution controls; and containing urban sprawl, among many others. SELC does not charge clients or partners for its services, relying instead on charitable gifts from individuals, families, and foundations.

TARA KOENIG, SWEETHAUS
sweethaus.com

Tucked just over the bridge on West Main Street in Charlottesville, Sweethaus is the perfect marriage of vintage and contemporary. Featuring shelves lined with large glass bowls brimming with candy in every shade of the rainbow, and a case packed with homemade cupcakes, the shop has an echo of an old-time mom-and-pop store, trimmed in the fresh colors and bright light of an energetic young business.

Tara and her husband, Billy, designed the space using reclaimed and antique materials, lending it a rustic, lived-in feel. This is especially true of the large dining area in the back of the shop, which features a comfy couch and chairs, a half-dozen tables for gatherings of all sizes and an inviting children's play area, all immersed in light that pours in from a wall of windows. In this space is also the Sweethaus event kitchen, where folks young and old can attend parties and gatherings that give them the opportunity to make and decorate their own cupcakes.

Be sure to watch for Georgia, Sweethaus' mobile cupcake shop, at local events and festivals!

KATE COLLIER & ERIC GERTNER, FEAST!
feastvirginia.com

When Kate and Eric launched specialty grocery store Feast! eleven years ago, the local food movement in Charlottesville was truly nascent; thus, Feast! ended up being on the front end of a very major wave, specializing in locally sourced foods from throughout Virginia.

"It's been really exciting to see all the young people that have gotten into the local food movement," Kate says. "There are many involved in the business of it, or they are supporting it. Especially young families—I think that paints a bright future." Through their work with the Urban Agriculture Collective of Charlottesville—where they volunteer with their son, Oscar—and their creation of Local Food Hub, Kate and Eric are trying to ensure that this wave of interest in locally produced food continues to swell and serve more people in our community.

Learn more about the Urban Agriculture Collective of Charlottesville at uaccville.wordpress.com and Local Food Hub at localfoodhub.org.